They call me "Obsessive Compulsive Miss Order" so I really thought I knew it all and more when it came to organization. Now, thanks to Karen Ehman, I'm even more obnoxious than ever! I'm also more peaceful, sane, and clutter-free. When it comes to managing your home, whether you're a neophyte or a sage, there is much to learn within the pages of this life-enriching book.

LISA WHELCHEL, AUTHOR,
CREATIVE CORRECTION AND
TAKING CARE OF THE "ME" IN MOMMY

"Reading a Karen Ehman book is like sitting down with a girlfriend over a cup of tea and solving life's problems. She's honest, fun, down-to-earth, and incredibly practical. Karen's unique twist is that she doesn't try to get you to do it her way—she helps you find your unique organizational style!"

JILL SAVAGE, EXECUTIVE DIRECTOR,
HEARTS AT HOME, AND AUTHOR,
GOT TEENS?

"This book will stay front and center on my resource shelf as the 'go to' book to getting and staying organized. Thank you, Karen, for being the organizational mentor I've always wanted."

LYSA TERKEURST, PRESIDENT,
PROVERBS 31 MINISTRIES, AND AUTHOR,
GOD'S PURPOSE FOR EVERY WOMAN

"Karen gives you what you need to become 'a woman on top of the organization pile.' She answers your dilemmas about how to declutter your life and home."

EMILIE BARNES, AUTHOR,
MORE HOURS IN MY DAY AND
101 WAYS TO CLEAN OUT THE CLUTTER

"On occasion, my ducks have not only not been in a row, but someone has stolen them! Karen Ehman skillfully, realistically, and delightfully explains the good news that all of us can organize differently with assured success while arming every woman alive with humor and a doable plan."

CINDY SIGLER DAGNAN, AUTHOR,
WHO GOT PEANUT BUTTER ON MY DAILY PLANNER?
AND *CHOCOLATE KISSES FOR COUPLES*

"Busy moms rejoice! Karen Ehman offers you guilt-free, custom-designed and family-friendly organization that really works! Karen's book gave me, a work-at-home mom of five, the ability to laugh at my own organizing disasters, encouragement to find solutions, and inspiration to be better prepared to answer God's daily call on my life."

GLYNNIS WHITWER, AUTHOR,
*WORK@HOME: A PRACTICAL GUIDE FOR WOMEN
WHO WANT TO WORK AT HOME*

"Karen Ehman rescues the overwhelmed by offering creative solutions for calming the chaos. Brimming with realistic and practical home-management ideas, readers are sure to find encouragement, avoid stress, save time, and enjoy more meaningful moments with loved ones."

GINGER PLOWMAN, AUTHOR,
HEAVEN AT HOME AND
DON'T MAKE ME COUNT TO THREE

THE COMPLETE GUIDE TO GETTING & STAYING ORGANIZED

KAREN EHMAN

HARVEST HOUSE PUBLISHERS

EUGENE, OREGON

Karen Ehman: Published in association with the literary agency of Alive Communications, Inc., 7680 Goddard Street, Ste 200, Colorado Springs, CO 80920. www.alivecommunications.com.

Cover photos © Dex Image, PNC/Digital Vision, Yo/STOCK 4B-RF/Getty Images; Digital Vision Photography / Veer

Cover by Dugan Design Group, Bloomington, Minnesota

THE COMPLETE GUIDE TO GETTING AND STAYING ORGANIZED
Copyright © 2008 by Karen Ehman
Published by Harvest House Publishers
Eugene, Oregon 97402
www.harvesthousepublishers.com

Library of Congress Cataloging-in-Publication Data
Ehman, Karen
  The complete guide to getting and staying organized / Karen Ehman.
     p. cm.
  ISBN-13: 978-0-7369-2074-2 (pbk.)
  ISBN-10: 0-7369-2074-9
  1. Mothers—Religious life. 2. Homemakers—Religious life. 3. Christian women—Religious life. I. Title.
  BV4529.18.E36 2007
  248.8'431—dc22
                                                    2007005542

Printed in the United States of America

08 09 10 11 12 13 14 15 / BP-SK / 11 10 9 8 7 6 5 4 3

To my oldest and dearest friend, Kelly Hovermale.

Here's to 25 years of helping each other get and stay orga-
nized—from planning our college's homecoming celebrations to
now being moms to seven children. Through it all you've offered
me ideas, encouragement, and the needed "atta girls" to keep me
plugging away and pointing toward God. I treasure our friend-
ship. I covet your prayers. My life is sweeter for knowing you.

ACKNOWLEDGMENTS

To my sisters (and some brothers) in Christ, both at Hearts at Home and at Proverbs 31 Ministries: Thank you for the avenues you provide for me to speak, write, act, and serve, but most of all, to eat dark chocolate!

To Jill Savage, Mary Steinke, and all the women on the publications team at Hearts at Home, and to literary agent Beth Jusino of Alive Communications: Thanks for your part in the creation of this project.

To the fantastic folks at Harvest House publishers: Thank you for believing in me.

To graphic designer Amber Fuller and Web site creator Vicki Hughes: How God dropped you both into my life is astonishing. Your work is top-notch, and you go above and beyond the call of duty. I am forever in your debt!

To Paul "Precious" White: You are our family's biggest cheerleader, and your thoughtfulness does not go unnoticed. Hang in there, buddy.

To dear friends Steve and Eileen Feldpausch: I appreciate your willingness to let the boys hang out at your farm on those occasional weekends that Mackenzie and I have a speaking engagement and Todd has to work. (And with eleven kids, I'm sure you don't mind two more!) You are a wonderful example of a godly and gifted family both in music and in ministry.

To my mother, Margaret Patterson: You are an amazing example of an intentional mom, and I have learned so much from you. Seeing you rely so heavily on God made me want to have a relationship with him too. Thanks, Mom. You're the best.

To my prayer team of Pastor Tim, Kelly, Suzy, Debi, Marcia, Mary, Marybeth, Marielle, Amber, Patricia, Tammy, Dorothy, Heather, and Dr. Jennifer: Thank you for covering my family and my speaking engagements in prayer. I feel and see the fruit of your labors constantly. I would never attempt this without you!

To my children: Mackenzie—Thank you for working on this project and serving as my personal assistant when I speak. I love watching you discover the ministry God has for you. Mitchell—Thanks for hauling my books in and out of the van without complaining. I always wanted a long-haired, guitar-playing son who loves Jesus. Now I've got one. Spencer—What a boring place our home would be without you! Your song-singing, joke-cracking, impersonating, story-telling personality makes Dad and me crack up! Thanks for my lucky writing sweater. I'm wearing it now! Although you all are normal siblings with the usual rivalries and occasional fights, you are also crazy about one another. It makes me smile.

To my husband, Todd: You quietly serve. You wordlessly love. Daily you model for our family what it means to be a true follower of Christ, even when no one outside of our four walls is looking. And after nearly twenty-five years, I still think you're hot!

And to my heavenly Father: Thank you for the forgiveness I don't deserve, the salvation I could never earn, and the promise of a glorious future with you someday, where there will be no more to-do lists, carpools, dirty dishes, or laundry. Then I can endlessly spend my time with the saints gathered around the throne singing praises to your holy name. I can hardly wait!

CONTENTS

• •

BEING ORGANIZED MEANS
BEING PREPARED

When it comes to organization, didn't becoming a mom kind of throw you for a loop? I mean, maybe you weren't a perfectly polished perfectionist when it came to your home and time, but most likely you were able to reasonably hold things together on the home front. If you washed the floor, it stayed looking shiny for at least a few days. Scrubbed the sink or scoured the tub? You wouldn't need to do that again for a week or two. Maybe you organized a bookshelf or tackled a pile of papers and then basked in the glory of having it all neat and tidy. I'll bet you even made it to your appointments on time, barring any unforeseen circumstances. And can any of you remember this glorious concept—doing laundry just once a week? Sigh.

However, something happened to throw off our timing, plunging us into a downward spiral of dejection and sending us tottering near the edge. What was it? Sickness? Calamity? Natural disaster?

Nope. It was one of two simple things. Either you finally received that long-awaited phone call from the adoption agency letting you know your precious child was waiting for you or one morning, upon rising, you discovered it. The stick turned blue!

Ahhh, yes...blessed motherhood. What an honor. What a privilege. What a headache! Now, just as we get all our ducks in a row, along comes one of our own little ducklings to completely knock them off the shelf, forcing us to start all over again. It's enough to make a grown woman cry. I know. I've gone through too many boxes of Puffs Plus to count!

But does this have to be? Are we moms destined to disorganization and disarray until that last duckling grows up and leaves our cluttered coop? Or can we moms still manage our homes in a timely and orderly fashion while in the midst of rearing kids? Can we not only *get* organized, but manage to *remain* that way in this hectic and labor-intensive season of motherhood?

A resounding yes! But the yes is directly dependent on our definition of organized.

I am convinced that moms, given the right tools and with plenty of proper motivation, can maintain a thriving, inviting, and relatively smooth-running home. Notice I did not say spotless. I made no mention of perfect. I'd never be so bold as to assert that it will come off without a hitch. But your life as a mom can be much more organized than it is at this moment.

How do I know? Because I've seen it happen for many moms I've interacted with. They have taken life by the reins and are determined to steer it toward order and quit whining about it.

But most important, I am living proof of it. While I went through an intense time of disorganization directly due to motherhood, now things clip along pretty well around our home. No, not 100 percent of the time. Anyone who asserts her life is perfectly organized every day of the year is either lying or has no life! I would never say I don't have times when it's bump and go. But usually our home functions relatively smoothly. Why?

Let me assure you it isn't because I am a Polly Perfectionist by birth. While I do lean more toward being a neatnik than a messy, I do *not* enjoy deep cleaning on a regular basis. I know some women who do. Me? I'd rather be off having fun! And it isn't because I have a lot of free time. I'm under just as many time constraints as the next gal. I have three kids and their activities as well as a hubby who'd like some of my attention more than once in a while. It isn't even because I'm just one of those obnoxious organized types who gloats and brags because order is so second nature to her. Why, then, am I usually able to be at peace with the balance of order and chaos in my life?

Two reasons: First, because after years of trial and error, I have a plan for my work, and I work the plan. And all the while, I am constantly reevaluating and readjusting that plan according to the season of the year or the season of my life.

Second, and more important, I have come to a bold realization: It's never going to get all done. You heard me. Stop the presses! Did you think this was a book that was going to show you how to do it all, all the time? Sorry. Dear Mom, you won't ever be able to do it all. The sooner you face that fact, the better. It won't ever be "all done." What a freeing thought. No, really!

Losing Your Life

When I first became a mom, I was taken completely aback when it came to organization. My firstborn was a colicky, clingy, high-maintenance little girl who never wanted to be put down. And being a first-time and well-meaning mom, well…I never put her down. I went from being in control of my time and my surroundings to being at my wit's end! My friend Debi tried to get me to see that it was a good thing. That I was "losing my life" in order to become the person God wanted me to be.

Hold it right there, lady. I'd signed up to become a mom; I wanted a baby. However, I did not remember the part about signing up to lose my life. I'd somehow missed the fine print.

Before motherhood I'd prided myself on being a gal with all my ducks in a row. I sought to impress others with how competent I was to organize the project or head the committee. In high school I sought to have the longest list of clubs, sports, and organizations participated in right there in black and white under my name in the senior yearbook. I reached that foolish goal. My list included 33 activities and was over two inches long.

This pattern continued through college and into my married life. But five years into the marriage I became a mom and completely lost it. All of it! My time, my identity, my schedule; yes, you could even say my life. Before, I could take charge of an event, plan a function, or assume the headship of the group and turn out something wonderful. Now I couldn't manage to take a shower or even get out of my pajamas before my husband came home from work for lunch at noon. Talk about being humbled!

I remember those first few years of motherhood, trying frantically to get to the end of my to-do list by the end of the day, a feat I usually performed with relative ease before becoming a mom. Now I couldn't even get halfway through. Not even a quarter of the way through. Was I doing something wrong? Was my list too long? What was the matter with me?

It never occurred to me that perhaps I wasn't *supposed* to get everything crossed off every day. In fact, I remember crying one day as I felt completely overwhelmed trying to "get it all done." It was also a very pivotal day in my life.

A Lesson from the Past

We had just returned from a visit to Frankfurt, Michigan, the town where my husband's Grandma Ehman lived in an adult-care home. The victim of a stroke years earlier, Grandma had regained use of one side of her body and walked with a cane. Her days now consisted of reading and watching television. She closely followed her beloved Detroit Tigers baseball team, writing down the statistics in a book as she watched or listened to the game. She tried to remain active and attend an occasional church dinner or ladies luncheon. Her days were unhurried, her existence simple.

While there, I had spied Grandma's to-do list on her dresser; it looked something like this:

1. Write Fred and Carol.

2. Call Doug and Shirley about Thanksgiving.

3. Watch ball game.

4. Ride exercise bike for 20 minutes.

5. Help set table for supper.

6. Read church bulletin.

7. Play cards with lady down the hall.

8. Listen to Don Ho record before bed.

Later, as I sat wallowing in my self-pity and lamenting that I never get my to-do list done, I suddenly thought about Grandma Ehman. I could honestly say she was the only person in my life who crossed off every single item on her to-do list each day.

But wait! What had Grandma said to me just the day before? *"Oh, how nice—you get to be home enjoying your children and watching them grow up. How much activity there must be at your house these days! I'll bet there isn't a moment of quiet. I'd give anything to have one more day with all my babies at home."*

It was then I began to realize I had become a slave to my list. Whether it was an actual printed piece of paper or merely the one I had crafted in my mind, if I didn't check off all the items each day, I felt like a failure. More crucially, I *acted* like a failure.

I needed to rethink my whole outlook on life as a mom. While performing a job in the workforce, lists are important. They provide direction. They keep us on task. They offer a means for measuring how our time was spent during our shift. But as a mom, life is different. Trying to approach motherhood like a job left me completely bewildered. I felt I was accomplishing little if my plans were thwarted and my list was left undone. In reality, God had plans much more important for me, involving things to do that often involved a hidden service for him. Endlessly rocking a feverish baby, holding a crying boy with scraped knees and a bruised ego, stopping to talk with a teen as she sorted out the issues of life or just wanted to chat about the latest hairstyles. In his eyes, these were all important actions he had for me that day. I never even had them written on my list.

Please don't misread me and suppose I am against lists and plans and being proactive. Not in the least! I have, however, had to adjust how I view to-do lists. They are no longer my taskmaster and I their slave. Instead, they are my personal Global Positioning System (GPS), pointing me in the right direction but allowing me to still receive a call from the Lighthouse asking me to alter my course for a while. And I still look for shortcuts that will allow me to get more accomplished in less time so I can savor the sweet moments in life, the ones that Grandma relived in her mind over and over again.

Back to the Drawing Board

When I first realized I had to make these changes in my life, I began to gather information, pick other women's brains, and read, read, and read some more. As I turned to those who in my estimation were skilled at not only handling their homes and time well but who used their time to love and serve others, I found a common thread:

Being organized boils down to being prepared.

Think about it. Mom #1 receives a call informing her that so-and-so just broke her ankle and needs a meal brought in, and this completely throws her for a loop. Through her maxed-out brain runs this line of thought: *Sure, I'd like to make a hot meal and take it over to Mary, but I don't even have anything planned for my own family to eat tonight. I suppose I could feed them what we're probably going to have, but fish sticks and French fries or cold cereal just don't seem right.*

Mom #1 has two choices. She can stop what she's doing, run to the store, and drop a boatload of money on a prepared meal to take to the family. Or she can politely, with guilt in her heart, opt out.

Mom #2 receives the same call. She, however, is not thrown into a guilty panic and forced to regretfully decline, nor does she dash off to the pizzeria to pick up a large pepperoni and a liter of soda pop to deliver to the family. She simply walks over to her freezer, pulls out a homemade chicken pot pie, a frozen layered strawberry salad, and some mocha brownies for dessert. Then she strolls to her desk and selects a simple pick-me-up card to sign and deliver along with the meal. She then calls the family in need and says, "I have your meal ready. Would you like it delivered fresh or frozen?" The entire process takes only a few minutes of her busy day.

What's the difference? Was mom #2 smarter? A better friend or superior homemaker? No. She just recognized that in this stage of her life, she would be receiving such calls on occasion. So she prepared in advance, knowing that most likely the call would come on an already hectic day. Because of her forethought and advance activity, she was able to meet the request in a calm, collected manner.

More Than Just the Boy Scout Motto

Do you have a Boy Scout in your home? My boys have not joined their ranks, but while growing up, my brother was a Scout for nearly a decade. Their motto, well-known for over a century, is "Be Prepared." Well, my desire is that this book you now hold in your hands will help you become prepared for whatever and whomever God brings your way. It's not designed to make you a "Wonder Mom" who can wow her friends and impress her acquaintances with her advanced organizational skills. Its goal is not to enable you to keep a spotless house. It isn't even designed to help you manage your time more efficiently. Its goal is much bigger than that.

Organization for organization's sake is a dead-end goal. Our goal simply must be about something higher. Ultimately becoming organized should be a means to achieve the ends *God* has for us. To touch lives for good. To point others to him. To be prepared for the work he has for us to do each day. Not to alphabetize our spice cupboard or label all of our children's clothing with different-color permanent markers.

Being prepared is all about enabling you to take care of the "have-to's" in life—the shopping, cooking, cleaning, child care, bill paying, and on and on—in an efficient manner. Then you can get around to actually performing the "want-to's" of life—spending unhurried time with your family, reaching out to a neighbor, reading that book you've been meaning to, taking a walk, writing a handwritten letter to encourage someone in your life.

We get to that place by being prepared, by taking care of tasks on the front end before the tasks do us in as we desperately attempt to play catch-up with life.

Which Comes First—The Duck or the Egg?

In this journey together, we are going to tackle both aspects of organization: managing your time and organizing your things. But which comes first? Are you able to get your home and possessions in order only when you have gotten your time under control? Or will you be able to get your runaway schedule under control only when you finally get your place clean and tidy? Which comes first?

In most cases, I have observed that although the two work hand in hand, most moms need to deal with their stuff first. Because so much of life takes place within their four walls during the childrearing years, women become easily defeated when constantly faced with piles of papers and loads of laundry and the general disorder that creeps into their lives. They never get out of the starting blocks. The minute you get an area under control, it just gets messy again. So why try? Might as well grab a Diet Coke, turn on a good movie, and escape for a while. Sadly, many moms do this to put off dealing with their cluttered lives. While it offers a brief and temporary reprieve (and there is certainly nothing wrong with enjoying a good movie now and then), in reality, it solves nothing. It only delays facing the mess.

Try as I might, ladies, I am simply not able to give you a slick, one-size-fits-all solution to getting organized. I wish it were that easy! But unless you're fortunate enough to be able to hire a maid, a cook, and a chauffeur for the remainder of your childrearing years, you're simply going to have to use your own brain and body.

First, we'll walk through your individual life. You'll use your mind to evaluate just what areas in your life you want changed. You'll think through finding your organizational personality, determining which areas of your home are out of control, where you're wasting time, and how you can change.

You see, it doesn't do any good to just pick up a book and try to replicate someone else's plan. That hardly ever works. Why else do you think you see so many books on organization in garage sales and dotting the shelves of secondhand stores? Imitating someone else's plan usually only works if you are also living the same life as the author. What I hope to do is offer solutions that fit your situation.

After using your brain to come up with your plan of attack, we'll begin to flex some muscles as we shuffle your stuff—some to the garbage dump, some to the local charity store, but most to a more logical place in your home. You'll be encouraged to get friends to help you tackle tough tasks—call it an "Amazon Women" group—so you don't get overwhelmed. When your stuff is stashed more neatly, you'll have more incentive to keep it that way—even with kids in the mix.

And as far as managing your time—I can assure you this book does not tout a rigid schedule. Schedules can be a guide or your GPS, but they should not be your boss. Sometimes they do more harm than good, especially for that mom who feels defeated if she gets even slightly off schedule. I have found what is more realistic and certainly more doable: have a flexible routine that allows for interruptions from God and ministry to others.

The difference between a schedule and a routine is this: A schedule must be done in order and at the exact time allocated. A routine, while done in order, isn't attached to a time frame. If you must interrupt your routine for a while, that's okay. You simply jump back in where you left off when the interruption is over. No need to fuss and fume. There was not a specific time assigned to your various tasks anyway. Women who live by strict schedules often put the clock or tasks before people. I once met a woman at a function who seemed to be in an immense hurry and was irritated by people who were attempting to chat with her after the event. When questioned about her seeming frustration, she said something like, "This meeting was supposed to end promptly by four o'clock, but it didn't. I needed to be on the road by four twelve because it takes me thirteen minutes to drive home, and I need to arrive home by four twenty-five because I am going to clean my oven at exactly four thirty so it will be done by five thirty-five in time for me to fix supper. Now I am completely behind schedule, and I am not happy."

Helloooo! Have you ever heard anything so crazy in all your life? Can you imagine being such a slave to a schedule? Having a strict, rigid schedule does not allow time for people.

However, being a mom with absolutely no routine isn't effective either. You're constantly sidetracked by the phone or Internet, and at the end of the day you may have connected with a lot of people but you haven't gotten any work done. No, a more balanced approach is to find your own flexible routine that allows for worthwhile interruptions.

Striking the Balance

I want to assure you that having children and being organized are not mutually exclusive. We simply need to strike the balance between structure and spontaneity. It will help, too, to train the little people in our lives to help us, not just because we want to see them work, but because it frees the whole family to enjoy life more.

Through the pages of this book, you'll meet a lot of people. First, you'll meet my daughter, Mackenzie, a formerly messy kid turned mostly tidy teenager. Occasionally, she will offer some advice from a young person's perspective—what works and what doesn't when it comes to getting kids to cooperate in getting organized. When the entire family is on the same page working as a team, this mission is more easily accomplished.

Second, you'll meet other moms in the "What Works for Me" sections who have been gracious enough to offer suggestions, stories, and ideas from their diverse lives. Because not all of you live lives similar to mine, I want to offer you a great variety of tried-and-true solutions to managing both your time and your home.

This book is designed to be read from start to finish s-l-o-w-l-y. You'll need to pause and ponder, to retreat and reflect. While you may want to jump ahead, thinking, *I wonder what it says about grocery shopping...or laundry...or...*, try to fight the urge. You'll gain the most benefit from reading this in its entirety, periodically stopping to do the exercises suggested. This will help you focus your efforts and zero in on the best game plan for your family.

So let not your heart be troubled! Together we'll walk through your life, evaluating the demands as well as delights that are a part of it. We'll come up with a plan for you to work at that will enable you to be prepared for whatever and whomever God sends your way. Do not suppose this will be an easy undertaking. I will try to make it simple—straightforward—but it will not be easy. Few things in life that are worthwhile ever are. But the results will far outweigh the effort required to get there. Are you ready to try? You can do it!

Points to Ponder

Here is where we begin to take steps that will help you craft your individual plan of attack when it comes to getting your home in order and your time under control. But just to make it a little easier on you, work through this next section in a quiet place where you can be alone. I want you to really think about the questions I am about to ask. So grab a cup of something to drink and steal away for a few minutes. The baby finally down for a nap? Great! Dad willing to take the kids to the park to play for a while? Wonderful! Could you drop the little darlings off at a friend's while you visit your favorite coffee shop? Perfect! You need to think clearly and without interruption as we begin to sketch out your personal and attainable goals in this area. Ready? Let's begin!

Write down the top three areas in your life that you most want to see changed in the realm of organization. These areas may have to do with time or with your physical surroundings. Perhaps it's a task like grocery shopping or menu planning. Maybe it's your ever-mounting piles of paper. Maybe it's your morning before-school routine. Don't think too hard; just write down the first three areas of frustration that pop into your mind.

Area #1

Area #2

Area #3

Now, describe how you are currently operating in these three areas. For each area, answer the following:

1. What are you currently doing (or *not* doing)?
2. What are the results?
3. How is this frustrating you?

Area #1
Current plan:

Results:

It frustrates me because…

Area #2
Current plan:

Results:

It frustrates me because…

Area #3
Current plan:

Results:

It frustrates me because...

Now, as you look back over these three areas, are there any obvious changes you know can be made? A simple example: Perhaps you fold laundry when your 15-month-old is playing on the floor in front of you. Thus your piles constantly are being overturned. What could you do differently? Put junior in a playpen with his favorite toys? Fold during naptime or early in the morning or after everyone else is in bed? What obvious solutions come to mind?

Area #1

Area #2

Area #3

Sometimes others see what we cannot. Are there relatives or friends in your life who seem to have these areas under control? Don't be shy or feel you are a failure if you ask for their advice. We are meant to live in connection with one another. Write down their names below and what areas they may be skilled at that you are having difficulty with. Beside their names write a few questions you want to ask them. Set a time to talk to them this next week.

Finally, write a list of at least three things you wish you had more time for. Three things that if the "have-to's" in your life were all taken care of, you would enjoy doing. Dream for a moment. If you had more disposable time, what would you do?

Good work. Now set this book aside for a while. You've gotten off to a great start. It will take time, but before too long you'll be on your way to a better organized, more focused you. Remember, we aren't shooting for perfect, flawless, or anything close. We aren't going to fool ourselves into thinking we're going to get it all done and have it stay that way. We know better. We're aiming to (1) find the rhythm that is ours—a flexible routine that allows for interruptions from God and ministry to others, and (2) seek to set the bar where it works for *our* families and lifestyles. Together we'll tackle both of these goals. You can do it! Be patient. You won't be perfect, but who would want to be anyway?

(2)

FINDING YOUR ORGANIZATIONAL PERSONALITY

Five-year-old Ryan was our next-door neighbor. A blond-haired, brown-eyed ball of energy whose favorite pastime was riding his bike—his rickety, red, girl's Schwinn bicycle that had been handed down through several cousins before making its way into Ryan's garage and heart. He proudly rode that bike up and down our block each afternoon. So imagine my surprise when one September day I happened upon Ryan kicking his beloved bike as it lay on the ground.

"What are you doing, buddy?" I questioned.

"Stupid bike," he murmured, still striking it with the toe of his tennis shoe. "Cool kids have bright-blue—mud puppy—dirt bikes, not some dumb ol' girl's bike from their cousins."

All of a sudden it dawned on me: It was Ryan's first day of kindergarten. And sure enough, at recess the kids had discussed what bikes they owned, and in Ryan's eyes his prized possession had suddenly turned stupid. His contentment had vanished.

Contentment: Country singers croon about it, and we women long for it; however, for many of us it seems just beyond our grasp. Why?

21

Comparisons: They deal a fatal blow to our contentment.

My house is just fine...until my sister builds one larger and more functional. My clothes are satisfactory...until I see the latest must-have fashions. Why, even my husband's not a bad guy...until I think of my friend's handy hubby who can build an addition on their house, while mine can barely fling a paintbrush.

You see, we're usually content with our Schwinn hand-me-downs—until we spy our neighbor with her new, bright-blue mud puppy.

The great playwright William Shakespeare said it fittingly in his work *Much Ado About Nothing:* "Comparisons are odorous." Do you know what that means? They stink! And if we wallow in comparisons long enough, we begin to stink.

This is never truer than in the area of time and home organization. What envy and strife can come when we compare ourselves to other women! Maybe it's that PTO mom who always seems to have it together. Her boys are certainly cleaner than yours. Her daughters have matching outfits and beautifully brushed hair sporting coordinated ribbons. And this mom herself? Not only is she a couple of sizes smaller than you, her outfits always look so put together, unlike yours (a pair of jeans out of the dirty laundry "paired" with a washed-but-still wrinkled shirt). And by the time she makes a remark about getting home to get the herbed pot roast and roasted garlic vegetables out of the oven in time to serve with her homemade raspberry truffle cheesecake, you've had it! You, on the other hand, were wondering if your family would mind having five-dollar pizzas for the third time this week.

Stop the comparisons! Some of the time, what we see is only a facade. So get your eyes off those seemingly perfect people. Look for the real ones instead. And most important, let's focus on *your* life and home for a while and how it can be improved. It will benefit not only those living within its four walls, but also those with whom you'll come in contact during the course of your days. And ultimately, it will make God smile as he sees you willingly accept the part he has chosen for you to play on this earth.

Taking Mommy Inventory

Okay, now that we aren't going to compare ourselves to others any longer, let's talk about your life as a mom for a moment. You've hopefully already identified three key areas that are causing you frustration. Now we're going to talk about three concepts as we seek to answer the following questions:

> What ticks you off?
>
> What makes you tick?
>
> What tickles you?

These three little questions are going to help us come up with a plan for your particular family. They will show us where you should set the bar when it comes to organizing your home. At the risk of sounding repetitive, I want to reiterate that this book is not about getting you to follow my slick system. It isn't trying to turn out cookie-cutter moms who run their homes in exactly the same way. Remember, trying to replicate someone else's routine will only leave you frustrated unless you live her same life. Your plan needs to be tailor-made for you.

What Ticks You Off?

First of all, what ticks you off? What areas of your home are causing you the greatest amount of displeasure and really getting on your nerves? In your mind, go through your entire home, top to bottom, and think about this question. You'll definitely have more than a few areas, and each woman's answer will be unique to her. Perhaps one gal cannot stand a messy garage. Her neighbor, however, is never really bothered by garage clutter because her garage is at the back of the house where no one sees it. Maybe another mom gasps at the thought of a junk drawer—one that holds pencils, paper clips, bottle openers, tape, and an assortment of other homeless objects. Her friend may think having such a drawer is part of the American way. Each mom will identify unique aspects of her home that tick her off. I'll walk you through one of mine.

First of all, I have a severe aversion to winter items—boots, hats, gloves, and such—being dropped just inside our side door by the little darlin's—bless their hearts—as they enter our abode. I don't know why, but it makes me completely blow my stack. I know I should be reminding myself what a joy it is to be a mom, how fortunate I am to have healthy children who can play in the snow, and how quickly the childrearing years fly by!

Well, let 'em fly! I am tired of all this mess. It irks me so, all these sopping-wet accessories. Why? Perhaps it has something to do with the fact that I spend 45 minutes getting everyone ready to trek outside to play, and they return 20 minutes later dropping all their saturated accessories on the floor. Since I did not want my children to grow up associating playing in the snow with mom wailing like a banshee and foaming at the mouth, I knew I needed to find a solution to my problem.

One day while in the organizational section of a department store, I happened upon a clever invention. It was one of those over-the-door pocket hangers designed to hold shoes. Suddenly, I had a brainstorm. I could use that contraption to hold my kids' winter things. It had five rows with four pockets in each row. Since the main structure was a thick, sturdy canvas and the pockets cotton mesh, I reasoned that the gloves, hats, and mittens could dry out while in the pockets. We even had five people in our family, so each person could have a personal row. Dad would be at the top and on down to Spencer, who was a toddler at the time and could certainly be trained to reach his row.

I snatched it up, took it home, and hung it on the back of our living-room closet door. Then I called an emergency family meeting. (It *was* an emergency. Mom's sanity was at stake!) I explained how this was going to work and what the consequences were for those who did not follow the plan. To my amazement, it worked! They liked having their own row in which to stash their stuff. And when winter was over, I converted it to summer storage. During our warm Michigan months, these pockets hold bottles of sunscreen, bug spray, deflated water wings, sunglasses, and other summer sundries. How simple!

You see, we all have areas in our homes that irritate us, ruffle our feathers, and cause our families to witness us behaving badly. But so seldom do we actually do anything about them. Instead, we continue to yell and scream and tell the brood to shape up and get with the program, all the while not realizing there isn't any program to get with.

I had a teacher once who defined insanity this way: "Doing what you've always done yet expecting different results." How true! We long for an area of our home to shape up, for an out-of-control behavior to suddenly come under control, but we never change our plan of attack. And when you always do what you've always done, you'll always get what you've always gotten. Every time!

By this definition of insanity, I know a lot of moms headed for a mental breakdown. We keep repeating ourselves, and our kids (and sometimes hubbies) keep repeating the same sloppy behaviors. It's insane. Enough already. Let's find some solutions!

Now, we are going to get a bit more specific than in the first chapter where I asked you to list your three biggest areas of frustration when it came to time and home management. We are zeroing in on the physical areas of your home. As I said, the first step to finding needed solutions is to ask, *What ticks me off?* So below, I want you to list at least five physical areas of your home that tick you off. Is it having nowhere to store off-season clothes? How about your piles of papers—school, extracurricular activities, and bills? Maybe it's the kitchen pantry with its half-empty boxes, stacked cans, and avalanche of Tupperware lids. Think about it. What areas of your home tick you off?

1.

2.

3.

4.

5.

Now, brainstorm solutions to these areas. Remember, don't just attack them in the same old way. Think out of the box. Perhaps this area is frustrating you because it's located in the wrong place in your home. Most homes are set up during one of the most stressful times in our lives—the first few days after we move in. You have no idea what your work patterns will be. Do you need to move any of these problem areas to another location? If so, circle or highlight that area and write down a different location better suited for the item. After doing so, walk over to your calendar and write down a time when you'll do this. Don't have a calendar? Put it on a sticky note and place it in a prominent place where you'll see it and take care of it soon.

What Makes You Tick?

On to the next question: *What makes you tick?* Which aspects of your life help you move along at a pretty good clip when it comes to being organized? Maybe it's having dinner all planned by early afternoon. It makes you feel on top of your game if you've thought about what you'll make for supper and made the necessary preparations. It pleases you to know your family won't be picking up a pizza *again* or making a quick run for other fast food.

What else makes you tick? Is it having your grocery list in a logical order so you don't have to keep running back up and down the aisles looking for something you skipped? What about your cleaning? Are you someone who likes a squeaky-clean floor? Does just knowing you mopped it make you feel good? (Remember, not everyone will be the same. Maybe your friend hates to mop and opts for the ceramic tile floor in a nice shade of "light-dirt smudge" with mocha-colored grout. Hey, mopping every other month would work for her!)

So list five things you like to see happen when it comes to your home:

1.

2.

3.

4.

5.

Let me ask you, *How can you build these into your weekly routine?* Where can you carve out chunks of time to ensure you are able to make these happen? Are there any products you need on hand to perform these tasks? What ways could your family help you accomplish these? Write out just how you'll execute these tasks on a weekly basis:

1.

2.

3.

4.

5.

What Tickles You?

Now, on to the fun one: *What tickles you?* My mother has used this phrase ever since I was a little girl. When she'd refer to something she really loved—an unexpected gift, a heartfelt action done on her behalf, a thoughtful phone call she received—she'd say, "Oh, that just tickled me to no end!"

Well, I want you to list some activities that tickle you. Perhaps it's reading that book your sister-in-law told you about. Maybe it's going to a coffee shop with a friend for mochas. How about writing a handwritten letter to a faraway friend? Are you a scrapbooker? Do you like to go for long walks or runs? What tickles you?

I want you to note five *simple* things that tickle you—things you can do on an ordinary day without wandering far from your house. For me it's sending a card to someone with a handwritten sentiment in it, playing catch with my boys, or lying on my daughter's bed for a chat while she listens to music. A simple mug of herb tea or flavored coffee savored while reading my Bible, a new book, or perusing a newspaper is always a pick-me-up too. How about you? What tickles you?

1.

2.

3.

4.

5.

Now, on to the more elaborate wishes. What would really tickle you if you could get away and do it either alone, with a friend, with your husband, with your kids, or with the family? Maybe you enjoy outlet-mall shopping, hunting for bargains for your family while you visit with a friend. Perhaps you and your husband want to take tennis lessons or learn how to ballroom dance. Perhaps it's the theater or a sporting event. What bigger activities or getaways refresh you?

For me, besides a weekend alone with my Mr. Wonderful, it's going to a bed-and-breakfast overnight with my best friend from college. Kelly and I would sip something hot, eat Weight Watchers meals and dark chocolate, and get caught up on projects we've been neglecting. You know, updating our address books and finally transferring all those numbers from sticky notes onto the pages. Then we'd go out for one nice dinner at a *real* restaurant that did not have a children's menu. On the way back to the bed-and-breakfast, we'd stroll along a quaint stretch of a brick-lined street with a lot of interesting antique and homewares shops. And in the morning, no alarm clock! We'd awaken at our own pace, steal away to a comfortable spot in the inn by ourselves to read our Bibles and pray before enjoying a delicious breakfast served by the innkeeper. Or if Kelly were unavailable, I'd sneak off for a similar weekend with my long-distance buddy Marybeth. Since we are both writers, we'd take our laptops and legal pads along, write and critique each other's work, and gab in between. Ahhh...just the thought of a twenty-four-hour period alone with a dear friend like that refreshes me!

Now your turn. Be specific. Don't hold back. Name some more elaborate activities that tickle you:

1.

2.

3.

4.

5.

These activities you have determined tickle you are going to be used in two ways. First of all, they'll serve as incentives—both daily and, at times, every so often. They will be the proverbial dangling carrots that will get you to be serious about keeping your home in relative order and your time in check. Because when you do, you'll take one of these small reprieves and special breaks from the mundane.

Then they'll serve their second purpose: rewards for jobs well done, applauding you, urging you on as you take in an activity that refreshes you, both body and soul. They'll be built-in rest stops along the way designed to spoil, pamper, and realign you in your quest to serve your family.

I can hear it now. The voices of some of you who assert, "But how selfish! I can't think of myself like that. I am a mom, a servant of my family. I really don't need any 'me time.' It just seems too self-serving."

I used to buy into that exact line of thought. For the first two years of motherhood, I never took time for myself. I mean never! My child was attached to my hip (or my chest!) nearly 24/7. Maybe I could make a quick trip to the grocery store while Todd watched the baby, but go away by myself for an hour or two? Go overnight somewhere with a friend for refreshment? Never! Todd and I didn't even have much "couple" time in that period in our lives. Sometimes my mom watched the baby while we wolfed down a sandwich at a nearby restaurant, but we had no regularly scheduled time alone.

I still remember the first time we tried to leave Mackenzie with a teen from our youth group when she was nearly two. She screamed and cried as we left, and then when we called to check on her 25 minutes later, she was still hollering! I dashed home, got the baby *and* the sitter, and we all enjoyed a nonromantic dinner out. So much for date night!

Now I know better. I have, though reluctantly at first, come to see the value in small rest stops both by myself and with my husband. I struggle much less with the blues and am more able to meet the needs of my brood when I do have a little "me time." I mean just a *little*. I'm not talking about flitting about town for hours every day, getting my hair or nails done excessively, or hanging out at the mall. I am simply suggesting small pauses, brief reprieves. And it concerns me when I see moms who never get them. Many are on the brink of physical and mental exhaustion, just like I was.

So begin now to schedule these times into your routine. From the first list—the simple, daily delights—aim to do one for at least a few minutes each day. I don't know about the rest of you, but knowing I'm going to have even a snippet of time to myself can keep me going full-steam ahead and reacting in a pretty agreeable manner to the delays, interruptions, and changes to my routine. When I started doing this, my kids were young, and I'd find a chunk of time during their afternoon naps. Even if it was for 15 minutes, I'd stop, make myself something to drink, and get my hands on something to read. It could be my Bible, a current book, or even a magazine of world news. Reading fills me up, diverts my attention (or focuses it back on God where it should be in the first place), and refreshes my soul. Those small breaks made such a difference in my day and in my attitude! Again, look over your schedule and start to build in some of these brief reprieves each week.

Then, on a different note, plan a bigger getaway, whether alone, with your husband, family, or a friend or two. Put it on the calendar. Go ahead and write it in bright-purple ink if that makes you happy. This will serve as an incentive and reward for the lifestyle changes you are going to make.

And what about the kiddos? Don't think you are the only one who is going to be rewarded for making an effort here. Grab your kids when you have a minute, and jot down some rewards they would like as individuals or as a family for helping mom in her quest for order.

Taking It Personally

Another important aspect of knowing just where to set the bar for your family is understanding your own personality. Are you a laid-back, take-life-as-it-comes kind of woman who is calming to be around but has difficulty starting and finishing projects? Are you a perfectionistic type who gives great attention to detail yet stresses and depresses when the plan doesn't go perfectly? Are you a take-charge mom who is proactive and driven, but your "whip it into shape" personality can drive your family away? Or are you the playful, fun mom who tends to have so many irons in the fire that the home and schedule go out the door, resulting in chaos, missed appointments, and late fees?

You see, any strength, carried to an extreme, can become a weakness. If you just ponder that thought for a while, I bet you can come up with oodles of examples. Each of these four personality types has inherent strengths. Left unchecked, however, they soon can negatively affect others in the home. We need to find balance. (That's why people instinctively attract and marry those with opposite personalities. Then, when married, the opposite personalities *attack* each other. Why? Because their personalities shift into their comfortable, dominant modes.)

We women need to be keenly aware of just how we are wired. And we need to make this work to our advantage when it comes to managing our time and our homes. For example, if you are a fun-loving sort who is easily distracted, making it hard to knuckle down and get any work accomplished, shoot straight with yourself. Trying to tackle tasks when you "feel like it" will not work for you. You won't ever feel like it. You'd rather play. Or when you're trying to get a task accomplished, say cleaning out the basement storage, you're easily distracted. You'll come across the box of old school yearbooks and, instead of just moving them to their new, logical location, you'll decide to pull them out and reminisce for a while. Two hours later, you realize you're only 20 minutes into your afternoon task!

A mom with this personality, since she tends toward fun, will need to be motivated and rewarded with fun. If you happen across that box of school annuals, handle it this way instead: Shriek with delight, give a giggle of glee, but then set that box aside. Tell yourself that *after* the job at hand is finished, or maybe after three hours of plugging away at it, you'll grab a Coke and that box and reminisce for a while. It also helps for this personality type to have another person hold her accountable. Have your husband check on you every half hour to make sure you aren't piddling around. Call a friend and tell her that if you do get distracted, you owe her a latte. Have her give you a call periodically that afternoon to help keep you on task.

What if you're the perfectionist? How can your personality best work for you? First of all, don't kill the job with details. Many women of this type are what I refer to as paralyzed perfectionists. Unless all the details are in perfect order, with flow charts and graphs and bars, they never start. They may do what they do flawlessly, but they do much less. Why? Because their motto is, "If it's going to be done, it has to be done right." Such a mom needs to relax her standards just a bit. Really evaluate if the added details are worth it in the end. Do you really *need* to have all your canned goods in alphabetical order? Perhaps. Maybe your family functions well this way. If so, more power to ya. If not, and instead you are continually frustrated because of "can confusion" in your pantry, and your family is sick of being chided for their lack of alphabetizing prowess, then...*lighten up, lady.* Find a happy medium. Maybe you can compromise and use this plan instead: all the fruits are on the left, the veggies on the right, and the soups and sauces in the middle. A detailed mom like this will need to make sure the results are worth the details, and where they are not, she will need to relax a bit for her family's sake.

The laid back, calm, cool, and collected mom has her own challenges—mainly that she can't seem to get any project started. Because she isn't a bark-out-the-orders sort, she herself needs an extra push to get going. Often, that push can come from her calendar. This mom will wait until she sees the birthday party looming in the near future to finally buy the needed gifts, supplies, and such. Because she is a take-life-as-it-comes gal, she simply sits back and hopes life will come at a manageable pace and in the right order. This dear mom will need to force herself to be proactive, learn to set goals, and then break them down into bite-size chunks and arrange them in logical order. (She can often do this with the help of a perfectionistic friend.) Although it feels foreign to her to be in charge, this mom must take charge of her schedule and projects before they take charge of her.

Finally, we have the task-oriented mom. She is on top of her game, all right. A real go-getter! Man, can she work. She blows into the room and blows everyone else away. While it may seem great to have a task-master like this—lots will get done, you know—this mom needs to realize that there are other people in the home. Actual living, breathing people. People with feelings. She needs to take a deep breath and take inventory of her to-do list, making sure she is taking into account the feelings and skills of others. When tasks are doled out, she needs to take note of the abilities *and inabilities* of family members. (No wonder junior couldn't take out that 90-pound load of trash. He only weighs 50 pounds and is in the first grade!) What this dear mom needs to work on is sensitivity. She already has a keen sense of what work needs to be done. Now she needs to be careful that her family is working together in a logical and caring manner.

Please be sensitive to the way God has wired you, but remember that everyone else in your home has been wired his or her own way too. We need to recognize our differences but remember we are all part of the same team. When we work *together* instead of against one another, life goes much smoother.

A Mother's Mission

I first began my adult writing career by taking over a newsletter for stay-at-home moms called *A Mother's Mission* that my friend Bonnie Davis had started three years earlier. It was a simple publication offering encouragement and ideas to moms who were serving God by loving and serving their families at home. I loved the title Bonnie came up with. Motherhood really is a mission. One of the definitions of *mission* is "a special assignment given to a person or group that may involve religious instruction or combat." That pretty much sums up my motherhood experience. Try as I might to fulfill the assignment God has given me to train these kids for life, somehow it still ends up involving a little combat.

Seriously, I think the reason that many of us moms struggle with feelings of inadequacy and loss of direction is that we fail to see that we're on a mission. We are undertaking a difficult and important series of tasks. Our focus must be clear, and our intent steadfast. To do this, we should come up with our own mission statements.

Many businesses and organizations have clear mission statements posted for all to see. My husband even discovered a Chicago taxicab driver who had a clear mission statement posted for his patrons to see. It was something like, "To provide my patrons with a clean, smooth, trouble-free, and timely drive to their intended destination while engaging them in lively and appropriate conversation." With that mission statement prominently posted and if he truly abided by it, is it any wonder he received bigger tips than the other cabbies who acted inconvenienced by their riders?

My favorite out-of-the-way eatery in nearby DeWitt, Michigan, is a place called Sweetie Pie Pantry. A retro combination bakery and snack bar, they offer fabulous vintage pies, cookies, muffins, and cakes, along with a sensational sandwich and salad menu. The proprietor, Linda Hundt, has a mission statement that reads, "Sweetie Pie Pantry's mission is: to celebrate love, tradition, and people through good food; to make our friends (customers) feel revered; to offer delicious, homemade pies, baked goods, preserves, and comfort foods, specialty merchandise, and cooking classes in a happy, loving, and nostalgic ambience; to honor tradition by means of honoring our elderly through community service projects and contributions."

I love eating at Sweetie Pie's! Not only do they have wonderful food, but they focus on their purpose. Making and serving yummy treats and eats is more than just a way to make money for them. It's a way to bless others in the process.

Well, Mom, it's time for you to craft your own mission statement. This will be a way to keep you focused on just why you're doing all this in the first place—the cooking, cleaning, scrubbing, wiping, kissing, cuddling, and counseling. In the appendix you'll find a reproducible form to photocopy on card stock and fill out with your mission statement. You may even want to add a related Bible verse.

Once it's written, post your mission statement in a prominent place to keep before your eyes. This will be a tangible reminder as to why you are doing what you are doing. Then when you are scrubbing that last pot of baked-on mess or mopping the floor for the tenth time that week, you can glance at your mission statement in your very own handwriting. I have found this really helps women remember that if you can't love what you are doing, at least you can remember that you love *why* and *for whom* you are doing it!

Here are a few sample mother's mission statements:

> To create an atmosphere of fun and love in our home while teaching my children to work hard, play often, and love God with all their hearts.

> To love and serve my family within these four walls, as I look toward the future when they will, in turn, serve others outside of them.

> To love, nurture, and discipline my children in a way that will point them to God and the plan he has for their lives.

If not right now, then sometime soon, turn to the appendix, photocopy the form, and write your own mother's mission statement.

There you have it. I hope these miniature "paper and pen" exercises have helped you begin to set the bar for your home and family. We aren't through yet. Next we'll tackle your surroundings—getting them clean and clutter free—well, actually in reverse order. We'll need to deal with your "stuff" first before we can begin any actual cleaning. But fear not, you can do this!

For now, relax and take a break. Go play a board game with your kids or take the baby for a walk in the park. Enjoy your family. Don't fret about the work to be done. It isn't going anywhere. Your kids, on the other hand... They'll be gone before you know it! Love on them for a while. This book will be waiting when you're ready to continue.

3

KICKING OUT THE
CLUTTER

• •

How many times in the past have you vowed to get your home in order, only to realize you had no idea where to start? Do you long to stop being overwhelmed by clutter, but just thinking about tidying up makes you want to lie down and take a nap?

If this is you, dear Momma, fear not! How I wish you and I could go out for a cup of something and come up with a plan of attack. Since that isn't possible, implementing the ideas in this chapter will have to do. I want to assure you that you can begin to climb out from under the clutter, dig out from beneath the dirt, and finally have this area of your home life under control.

I am not a major clean freak, but I do want my home to have order to it. I'd like to be able to locate items when I need them. I prefer not to have crumbs and crusties caked on my kitchen counters. And I find most moms long for the same things. While we wish for a clean and tidy home, what is needed first is a system to combat our clutter.

The Starting Block

When attempting to combat the clutter that has crept into your home, don't you feel like an airplane with nowhere to land? You circle your living quarters trying to find a place to start. You might even pick up some items and tote them to another location. But this isn't really dealing with your stuff. What you may need is to set aside some time, maybe a lot of time, to put your home through a good old-fashioned decluttering!

I first wrote about this concept in my book *A Life that Says Welcome: Simple Ways to Open Your Heart and Home to Others*. I am firmly convinced that many more families would open their homes to others if their homes weren't in such disarray. One of the wonderful benefits from attaining and maintaining order in your home is that you will no longer be embarrassed by its condition.

Decluttering has become a regular practice for my husband and me over the past twenty years. I first learned the basics of it from my mother who can clean circles around any other mom I've ever seen. I modified her system in college and continued to read anything I could get my hands on about this subject. (I've listed my favorite resources at the end of this chapter.) What has resulted is a method of decluttering that we follow about twice a year. It has been a huge part of our family's quest to keep our home's contents at a bare minimum and fight against the accumulation of unwanted earthly trinkets. For many moms, this can be the starting point they are looking for. I hope it will be for you! And I want you to know that our kids have pitched in and helped with this mission, starting from about the age of four. I say the sooner you train them to help around the house, the better.

Decluttering Basics

So here's how this works. First, you'll need five boxes, bins, or laundry baskets. They will hold items that you come across that belong somewhere other than where they are at the moment.

Label the first box *Put Back*. Inside of it place a small lidded container such as a shoebox or plastic tote. The big box will be used to collect the items that are currently out of place in your home. The smaller container will hold items such as pens, pencils, barrettes, and coins so they don't get lost in the bigger box.

Label the second box *Take Back*. This will corral all those items in your home that don't belong to you and need to be returned to their owners. You know, library books, rented DVDs, a shoe that your son's friend who spent the night last week left....

The third box will be used for garbage. Label it *Toss* or *Trash*. Line it with a garbage bag so when it becomes full, you can tie it up and transport it to the trash can. If you are a family that recycles, you can also have a box or bin for that purpose too.

Next, you'll want to have a box for those items that are still in good shape but no longer needed or wanted. Label this one *Charity* or *Garage Sale*. You can even place price stickers on your things at this point if you'll be holding a sale. If you'll donate your belongings to a charity or homeless shelter, as a box fills up, seal it and put it in your vehicle to be dropped off next time you are near a donation center. Phone first to inquire about their hours of operation and any stipulations they may have. While there, pick up a donation receipt for tax purposes. If you are a computer fan, check out the software *ItsDeductible*. It enables you to figure out your own deduction for donated items.

The last box in the bunch will be labeled *Nostalgia*. More on this in a minute.

Before starting, please determine that you'll be ruthless. Promise yourself that if you haven't used it, worn it, or enjoyed looking at it in the past year—then you're going to let it fly!

Haul your boxes into one room of your house. Pick one that holds the least clutter. Position the boxes in the middle of the floor. Beginning in one corner of the room, pick up an article, and ponder the following:

Is this item out of place? Place it in the *Put Back* box.

Does this item need to be returned to someone or somewhere? Into the *Take Back* box it goes.

Is this item in such dire shape that it's no longer usable? Then place it in the *Toss* box. If it's made of metal, glass, paper, or plastic, it goes in the recycle bin if you are going to add this step.

Is this item in fine shape but no longer needed by anyone in our family? Into the *Charity* or *Garage Sale* box it goes.

Is this item no longer needed by anyone in our family, but one of my children (or my husband) is so attached to it that if I pitch it now, they'll be emotionally damaged for life, and, yes, someday they will be on national TV spilling their guts to Dr. Phil about my cruel actions? Then into the *Nostalgia* box it goes. Each member of your family can have a Nostalgia box for favorite "keeper" items. I like to attach a note to the item such as "You wouldn't fall asleep without this stuffed turtle by your side" or "You carried this little lunch pail on the first day of school."

Continue making a sweep around the entire room, following the same procedure with each item you encounter. Check every drawer, shelf, and closet. Make certain you are taking inventory of everything you own. Be ruthless! When any box is full, empty it—put back the out-of-place items, put return items near the front door, throw out the trash bags, put giveaways into your car or garage (for the sale), and transfer the nostalgia items to a box that can be placed in permanent storage. What seems like an overwhelming task will soon gain momentum toward completion.

Don't forget to have a snack on hand. Taking a break every once in a while is a shot in the arm that helps keep you plugging away. Crank up some music you enjoy or pop in a book on CD to help the time pass more quickly. And if you are like me, you'll discover that this concept works best when following the buddy system. Clutter-busting is easier with a friend who is, unlike you, not emotionally attached to your stuff. She will help you decide objectively what you should keep and what you should pitch, give away, or sell. When you come to the electric knife Aunt Tillie gave you ten years ago that you never use, your friend will give you the courage to get rid of it, offering assurance that Aunt Tillie will not suffer irreparable harm because of your decision.

You might want to start by doing only one room a day, especially if your home is in pretty cluttered condition. Maybe you'll shoot for two or three rooms over the course of a long weekend. Even taking small steps, in a matter of a month or two you'll be done. It may take longer if you have a pack rat in your brood.

Taming the Little Pack Rats

Our daughter, Mackenzie, used to be the biggest little pack rat around. I'd get so annoyed at her when she was a preteen because of all the "junk" she insisted on displaying in her room. She placed all her lotions, perfume bottles, lip glosses, and such in rows on her desk. She hung all her many purses, backpacks, and bags on a pegboard. Other things were strewn about. She simply had to make sure all her belongings were in plain view, and it drove me absolutely nuts.

I, on the other hand, like to see nice, clean, simple counters and desktops. Give me a kitchen counter with a nostalgic antique bowl of plain fruit or a desktop with a beautifully framed picture of my family and a vase with a single flower, and I'm good to go.

Mackenzie and I had numerous run-ins over her habits, and I would often toss her "trash" when she was out of the house. She'd return home and become upset to the point of tears when she saw what I'd done. I'd give my "you keep too much junk" lecture, and our relationship became more and more strained. I knew I needed a solution to this dilemma.

If you, too, have a little pack rat in your brood, it will take some extra effort on your part to get him or her to cooperate in your decluttering project. But with a bit of cleverness, it can be accomplished. First, let her know just what a "clean room" actually means. She's just a kid; she doesn't know. Gently and quietly explain it to her. Don't yell; it doesn't work.

Some kids, especially preteen girls, can't quite grasp this concept of clutter control. Why? It's because their "stuff" is an important part of their personality, an extension of who they are. One day I finally wised up to this fact and quit attacking my daughter's person. I put on one of her favorite CDs and applied some sparkle lip gloss. Then we began a calm, but fun, decluttering session where we both talked honestly.

She vocalized her hurt over the way I had been so demeaning to her by constantly riding her about all her junk...uh, I mean her wonderful treasures. I expressed how it bothered me to see her possessions strewn all about, especially due to the fact that her bedroom door opened directly into our living room.

We came up with a few compromises and dashed off to the department store to buy some fun baskets and bins. This way she could arrange her treasures in baskets instead of displaying each little item. This was actually the beginning of a big turnaround for her. She decided that she liked organizing. She saw how instead of displaying some of those extra possessions she owned but never used, she could turn them into a profit at our garage sale. Then she could pool the money to buy one bigger item she really wanted.

Getting on Clutter's "Do Not Call" List

Once your home is thoroughly decluttered, you must hold fast. Don't return to your unhealthy patterns of junk collecting. Stay away from garage sales if you are tempted to purchase things you don't really need just because they are such a great deal. You must also learn to be firm with the well-meaning people who insist on giving you their spare stuff. Politely decline. Keep Grandma away from the dollar store. Tell Uncle Louie you are severely allergic to souvenirs. Let your friends know you have enough hand-me-down clothes, thank you very much...unless you really need them.

Okay, Mom, no more excuses. You have a system that will work. Now you need only to gather your tools and block out the time. Just think of the calm that will flood your life when you truly get your living quarters into proper shape. You'll feel more like having others over. You'll feel more like staying home for a quiet evening. Everybody wins when your home is devoid of clutter. So grab your decluttering boxes. It's time to begin!

Little Tips for Your Little (and Not So Little) Ones

Having trouble getting the little people in your life to keep their belongings in their proper places? Here are a few ideas that can help you kick the clutter habit and lose that cluttered look in your home for good.

Let your kids have some say in deciding how to organize their stuff. Of course they won't do it the way you would, but that's okay. Or, if you are a perfectionistic parent who simply can't stand disorder, at least let them decide about areas you won't see—the setup of their closet, what drawers their clothes will go in, which drawers in their desks will be used for what. I have found that two of my children have better and more logical locations in mind than I did. The third? The "open and chuck" method of organizing works for him. Open the closet and chuck in your coat and hat; open the drawer and chuck in your clean, unfolded clothes.

Teach your kids the value of the phrase, "Don't just put it down, put it away!" I have heard this phrase uttered by numerous organizing experts over the past twenty years, and my kids have been able to recite it verbatim since they were tots. Teach them where their toys, books, treasures, and trinkets reside, and then train them to put the items back where they live. Especially drive this home when they return after a day at school, a sport's practice, or other outing. Don't you find that wherever your kids' point of entry into your home is, that's where you tend to find the most clutter? They drop their books, papers, hats, scarves, mittens, everything…and dash off to get a snack or flop on their beds to phone a friend. Insist they take the extra one to two minutes it takes to actually walk their items to their proper locations. This is a great clutter-busting tool!

Consider going on a clutter-busting journey with your kids. Children today have way too many earthly belongings. I fear we are trapping our kids in a lifestyle of "stuff" when we let them accumulate scores and scores of possessions. Occasionally spend some one-on-one time with your kids decluttering their drawers, closets, and desks. Also check the basement, toy room, and garage. If you aren't having a garage sale, donate these items to a charity or homeless shelter. Be on the lookout for toys your children no longer play with, games they no longer enjoy, and books they haven't read in years. Be sensitive to the fact that the item may be something they no longer use but are still attached to, such as a special stuffed animal or doll. Place these items in Nostalgia boxes and assure them you will not get rid of them. They can retrieve them periodically, and someday, when they move out of your home, they can take their Nostalgia boxes with them.

Occasionally reward your brood when they are making a concerted effort to keep the clutter at bay. Make them a treat or take them to the dollar store and let them pick out something either consumable or useful. (You don't want any more junk, remember?) Play a game with them. Announce you will do their chores for today, and then kidnap them and take them to the park to play. Do whatever speaks love to them!

30-Minute Clutter-Busters

Got 30 minutes to spare? I know, moms *never* have time to spare. So get up early, stay up late, find 30 minutes when you're on hold with the insurance company. Just grab half an hour and tackle one of the following tasks, some of which can actually be done in less than 30 minutes.

1. *Dump out one drawer in the kitchen.* Sort the contents into three piles: out of place, throw away, and put back. Wipe out the drawer. Replace wanted items. Put those that are out of place back where they

belong and pitch the throw-away items. If you find any items that are unwanted but still in good shape, place them in a box to be donated to charity or sold at your next yard sale.

2. *Balance your checkbook.* Go online or use the telephone teller to see which checks have cleared and which deposits have been made; then do the math to get your current balance. *Warning:* If it has been a long time since you've done this, it will take more than 30 minutes. If you do this every week or two, it will take much less time.

3. *Purge your purse.* Dump the contents onto the floor. Get rid of trash. Organize your money. Stash your receipts somewhere where you'll be able to locate them when needed. And consider getting a smaller purse. If you buy a big purse, you'll be sure to fill it. *Think small!* A "clutch on a string" type purse with space for a cell phone should do the trick. You can always keep this inside a larger tote bag or diaper bag if you want. It will be easier when shopping if you keep your main purse small and its contents narrowed down to the essentials.

4. *Clean your counters.* Move everything to one side of your kitchen counters. Wipe thoroughly. Move everything to the other side. Wipe the second half. Place it all back where it belongs.

5. *Disinfect your doorknobs.* This is likely the most germ-infested area of your home. Everyone touches the doorknobs, but no one cleans them. Experts say to give them a good rubbing with a disinfectant wipe every so often.

6. *Clean out your fridge.* Pull everything out onto the counter. Wipe down the inside. Replace only what is

not out of date. Pitch the rest. If any items are near the expiration date and not going to be used soon, freeze if possible.

7. *Clean out the freezer.* Use the same method of attack for the freezer. Discard anything that is out of date and no longer safe or tasty to eat. Can you say "freezer burn"? I knew you could.

8. *Mind the medicine cabinet.* Check the dates on all your meds, and decide which ones must be tossed. Rid the cabinet of any lotions, shampoos, and products you don't need. Wipe the shelves down and replace only what you're keeping. I do this twice a year when the time changes. That'd also when we check our smoke-alarm batteries.

9. *Organize the hall closet.* While you may not be able to make a dent in a large bedroom closet in 30 minutes, you might be able to straighten up a simple coat closet. Empty it, sweep it out, and wipe down any shelves. Hang the coats back up and reposition other hats, gloves, boots, and such. Consider getting plastic totes to keep like items together, further organizing the contents. Get rid of what you don't need.

10. *Purge the pantry.* Remove all canned and boxed goods from your pantry shelves. Throw away what is outdated. Make a pile of what is still good but your family won't likely eat. Donate this to a local food bank or homeless shelter. Replace items in an order logical to you. Sometimes, see if you can eat for a week with only the items you find in your pantry. I've invented some recipes this way. Go online to find recipes that pair items you have on hand. Shop for only what fresh items are needed to round out your meals. You'll save a bundle on your groceries that week.

11. *Fix the fixtures.* If you have light fixtures that need dusting and cleaning, take care of them now. If the fixtures have many globes or tulip-shaped glass cups, run them through a rinse cycle in the dishwasher. Dry and replace.

12. *Add an address.* Transfer any addresses from sticky notes, letter envelopes, and Christmas cards into your address book.

13. *Rearrange your recipes.* Take a look in your recipe files, and toss any cards or cutouts you don't use. Rearrange what's left. If your recipes are in great disarray, this may take more than one 30-minute block. If so, find another friend who has the same problem. Take your recipes, meet her at a coffee house, and have an "Amazon Women" session to get your recipes in order. I did this one night, placing them all in a three-ring binder with full-size page protectors for magazine cutouts and pages designed to hold individual photos for the recipe cards. I made sections for main dishes, side dishes, desserts, and miscellaneous. When I'm cooking, if something splatters onto the recipe, it can be easily wiped off.

14. *Give a movie review.* Sort through your videos and DVDs and pluck out any your family no longer watches. Save old-time favorites for nostalgia if you have a child who is particularly fond of one. Give the rest to another family who would enjoy them.

15. *Spit-shine a shelf.* Take time to pick through just one shelf in the garage or basement, ridding it of unwanted items and leaving it neat and tidy. If you do one shelf a day, that area will gradually get decluttered.

16. *Give thanks.* Anyone you've been meaning to write a

thank-you note to? Do it now. And to make it easier in the future, place some thank-you notes, stamps, return address labels, and your address book in a basket near your sofa or in a tote bag you can take to the doctor's office or carpool line. Grab it often to jot a note of thanks or encouragement to someone.

17. *Sort socks.* Have a basket or bag with single, lonely socks that have lost their mates. Dump the bag and pair up any matches. Better yet, pay a child a nickel a pair for any matches he can find.

18. *Peruse your porch.* Take a look at what others see when they knock on your front door. Does your front window need washing? The porch need sweeping? Are there cobwebs that could do with a good knocking down? Take a little time to make the entrance to your home look presentable.

19. *Deal with your drains.* Pour some baking soda in your kitchen-sink drain. Next, douse it with a little vinegar. The resulting bubbling action will freshen it up. Or pour some clog-removing liquid down the bathroom sink and tub drains to prevent hair clogs in the first place.

20. *Fiddle with your files.* Remove three or four files from your filing cabinet. Look through them and make sure the contents are still worth keeping. If you find manuals for appliances you no longer own or outdated paperwork, toss or shred them now. Doing this regularly keeps your files up to date.

The Bookshelf

Here are some tried-and-true books that will help you in your quest for clean and order. Pick up a copy for more solutions to maintaining a well-ordered home.

- *Cleaning Up the Clutter* and *More Hours in My Day* or almost any book by Emilie Barnes. Her books are full of wonderfully doable ideas and are so inspirational!

- *Speed Cleaning* and *Clutter Control* by Jeff Campbell and the Clean Team. For a free catalog of their helpful products, call 1-800-717-CLEAN (2532) or visit them at www.thecleanteam.com.

- *Is There Life After Housework?* and *The Cleaning Encyclopedia* by Don Aslett—this gentleman is a professional as well as a complete cutup. Talk about good, clean fun!

- *Secrets to Getting More Done in Less Time* by Donna Otto. This handy volume addresses nearly every aspect of organization with understandable tips and straightforward strategies.

• • • • • • • From the Heart of a Kid • • • • • • •

I think we kids sometimes need to put ourselves in our moms' shoes for a minute. We need to think how hard it would be to keep the house clean while doing laundry, dishes, and making dinner. We should imagine that mom just cleaned out an entire room, and then one of us kids drops our junk in it a half hour later. For us kids, it would be like us building the coolest Lego tower ever, only to have our mom come right along and kick it all down.

When I was younger, I used to argue a lot with my mom about my hair not being brushed, my homework not being finished, and all the other normal things that kids and moms sometimes fight about. But the worst thing was my room. I was the messiest kid you have ever met! I kept everything. I'm talkin' *everything!* My younger brothers and I would go on a walk, and I would find a bottle cap. I would keep it forever, stuffed under my pillow. Pretty soon the junk began to really pile up, which drove my mom bonkers. It wasn't until later that I learned the importance of truly decluttering (as my mom calls it) my room.

What really got me motivated was when I turned thirteen. For a birthday present, my parents, a bunch of my friends, and all their parents all came over and pulled a "while you were out" on me. This means they totally redid my whole room while I was away for the weekend. They painted it a pale lime green and decorated it in a retro theme with a comforter set and curtains I had been eyeing all year long. They even hung neon-colored beads on my door and placed a lava lamp on my dresser. It was an awesome surprise! But this really got me wondering, *How am I ever going to keep my room this way?* I knew I had to change, and finally I actually wanted to.

This was the starting point for me to quit being a messy kid and start taking some responsibility for the look of my room. If you were to see my room now, you would never believe the same person lives here. Even my closet, which no one sees, is usually neat and tidy. Not to say I'm never messy. But for the most part, my room is clean. I have to work to keep it this way, and so will your kids.

Here are some ways I keep my room clean and decluttered. Maybe they will help other kids get started too. Let your kids read this section...or read it to them.

- Make it a habit once a week to go through your room and gather up all the little things lying around that you don't really need anymore: things like school papers, broken toys, bent baseball cards, earrings that are missing a match, old wrist bands from summer camp. Throw away or recycle these items.

- At night, before climbing into bed, spend just five minutes putting away your toys or those clean clothes you have been stepping over for three days now. This way you don't have to do it when your friends call and want you to go play outside with them. Besides, your mom will be more likely to let you go out since you showed her some respect and did what she asked you to.

- If your mom lets you have a snack in your room, clean up afterward. This will make your mom extremely happy. Also, remember to thank her for letting you eat a snack in your room!

- This one is my favorite. Put on some good music and just have fun. Work is only work if you make it so. Make it fun, and it won't feel like work. Yep, I say find some good clean music to clean your room to.

- Most of all, learn a phrase my mom says often at our house: "Don't put it down, put it away." If we put our things away when we are through using them instead of just dropping them on the floor, it saves us time and our moms some major headaches. (And haven't ya ever noticed that moms are much more fun when they are headache free?)

☺ Mackenzie

$$4$$

MAXIMIZING EFFICIENCY
IN EVERY ROOM

• •

Doesn't it feel good to have kicked out the clutter? There will be times when you need to do a dejunking again. We do it twice a year to keep our clutter at bay.

While you were on your dejunking journey, I'll bet some of the following thoughts wafted through your mind: *Why is this item stored here? I wonder if it would be smarter to rearrange this pantry (or medicine cabinet or junk drawer or closet)? Why did I put this stuff on the main floor instead of upstairs?*

When you begin to reduce your clutter, you also begin to clear your brain. Now you can see that having extra "stuff" was only half the problem. The other half is that your home is set up in an illogical manner.

As I mentioned earlier, most of us set up our homes and decide where we'll stash stuff during a very hectic and stressful time—the first few hours and days after we move in. Although we might surmise that this should go there and that should go here, we really haven't lived in our homes long enough to know what our work patterns are. This is especially true in our kitchens.

In order to alleviate major headaches when it comes to food storage, preparation, and serving, we must have our kitchens set up in a user-friendly manner. I know from experience! I spent way too many months (if not years) trying desperately to function in a kitchen that was not momma friendly. I complained all the time about it: "It's way too small!" "Who designed this room anyway?"

While some of that was true—it was a small and not-too-cleverly designed room—the biggest problems were the places I stored my stuff. They often didn't make sense. Cookbooks stored over the top of the stove? Watch that belly when the water's boiling and I need to get out my favorite recipe for pasta. My spices were neat, but they weren't organized. A common misconception among moms is that the two terms are interchangeable. They're not. Just because something is neat does not mean it's organized.

We joke about the neatnik mom who has all her spices in ABC order. I actually had this setup in the house I'm speaking of. I had a large spice cupboard mounted on the wall. It was a beautiful sight: all my jars lined up in a row, willingly obeying me. Yep, alphabetized to a T: allspice, basil, cinnamon, dill…you get the picture. The only problem was that my spice rack was nowhere near the stove I cooked on or the counter where I typically baked. When I needed to grab an Italian spice such as basil or oregano, I had to turn and walk several steps to get to the cupboard, open the door, and retrieve the spice. If I was baking and needed ginger or cloves, I had to trek even further to my beloved, neat spice cupboard. What a pain!

I finally came to the realization that I needed to part with my precious piece of kitchen finery. So I thought through my kitchen in logical order and plotted out my traffic patterns—where I did what I did. I concluded that I didn't have to have all my spices in one location. After all, I used them in two locations. And I had a third category of spices that I used only occasionally. These were my summer canning spices: alum, turmeric, dill, cilantro, and kosher salt. What should I do with these?

Here's what I decided. I'd place my cooking spices in a cupboard that was right next to my stove. For my baking spices, I chose a bottom shelf of a cupboard just above the place where I had the most counter space to mix batter and dough. And the canning spices? I sealed those up in a small plastic tote and shuffled them off to the basement for storage. I only needed to retrieve these once a year when it was time to can pickles or salsa.

Doing this alleviated the headaches I had been experiencing due to my mislocated spices *and* freed up much-needed kitchen space. You see, while on my spice-reorganizing quest, I noticed other items that I used only once a year. So away went the holiday cookie cutters, the fancy birthday-cake platters, the candles and caketop decorations, and the seasonal table runners and tablecloths. I found turkey roasters I used twice a year and fluted mini cake pans I only used at holidays. Once I shuffled all this stuff out of my kitchen and into basement storage, I gained space. Hooray!

You can do the same too. As we walk, room by room, through your house, we'll be asking questions that will help you reorganize your home according to your work (and play) patterns. For each section, you'll answer a series of questions and then record what action steps you'll take in this area. Don't let this overwhelm you. You won't be reorganizing these rooms over one weekend. It will take time. And if you have more rooms than the ones listed (say, two bathrooms instead of one), you'll need to record answers for these rooms in a separate notebook. And please remember: This is just the beginning exercise. The following chapters contain lots of ideas for how to store and stash your stuff. For now, I want *you* to begin the evaluation process on *your* home. After all, no one knows it better than you. Let's see what solutions you can offer before we go further.

Living/Family Room

As the name suggests, the living room should be a place where living takes place. A family room should have room for the family. But what are the conditions at your home? Are these rooms in the shape you'd like them to be? Answer the following questions and record your responses in the space provided.

1. How would you rate this room on the organizational scale, with 10 being functional, logical, and relatively tidy, and 1 being utter chaos and clutter?

2. What are the normal activities that take place in this room? Do you watch television, play games, work on the computer, read…?

3. Are there any items that should be moved out of this room? Would the television work better in a finished basement room, freeing up the living/family room for computer work or quiet reading? Maybe the reverse is true. Is "junk" causing you distress and dismay because it's making the room an uninviting place to be? List the items that should be moved elsewhere, along with the locations you'll try keeping them in.

4. Is the furniture arrangement working for you or frustrating you? What could you do differently?

5. What about clutter? Do you have piles of newspapers, magazines, and junk mail littering the room on a daily basis? What could you do differently? Could you purchase a big, rustic basket to place the papers and magazines in, and then make a habit of discarding them once a week or once a month?

6. Is there anything else that is not working when it comes to this room? How can you change this?

Kitchen

This room causes moms the greatest amount of stress. No room is used more than the kitchen. If this room is not arranged in a user-friendly manner, it will cause you great grief. And when the kitchen causes you grief, it drives you to the phone to order pizza or fast food. Use this section to help streamline your kitchen.

1. How would you rate this room on the organizational scale, with 10 being functional, logical, and relatively tidy, and 1 being utter chaos and clutter?

2. What are the current frustrations when it comes to your kitchen? Do you lack cupboard space? Counter space? Are your pots and pans no longer functional with their broken handles and loose knobs? Are there any tools you don't have and need to get your act together in the kitchen?

3. How can you solve some of the dilemmas you just listed? What could you do to free up some counter or cupboard space? Are there items you need to save up for that will alleviate some of your kitchen hassles? Consider asking for some of these for Christmas or your birthday.

4. Take inventory of the way your cupboards are arranged. Actually walk over to them, open them one door at a time, and give them the once-over. Are there things in your cupboards you no longer need or use? Pull them out, place them in a box, and donate them to charity. Or if you'll be having a garage sale,

seal them up in a box until your sale time. If you have items you use only seasonally or occasionally, think of another location in your home where you could store these and retrieve them when you need them.

5. How about your dinnerware, glasses, and silverware? Are they stored in the most logical places? Are your glasses near the sink? Are your plates, forks, knives, and spoons easily accessible when it's time to set the table, as well as when it's time to take them out of the dishwasher or sink drainer and put them away? What about your pots, pans, cookie sheets, and muffin tins? Are you happy with where these are stored? Does it make sense to move them to a new location?

6. Now, how about your pantry? Is its organization working for you? Are your canned goods and boxes and bags in the spots that make sense? If not, where can you move them to?

7. What about cleaning supplies, mops, and brooms? Are these taking up precious space in your kitchen? If you don't have ample room to keep them here, is there space in the hall closet or basement or garage corner where you could place them?

8. Now let's talk trash. Kitchen trash, that is. What is your plan for garbage disposal? Do you keep a small trash can under your sink, a large one out in the room, or perhaps one of each? Is this working for you? If you just have a small one, does it get full too quickly, causing you constant grief? Should you switch to a

bigger one? If you are a family who recycles, what is your plan for those glass bottles and tin cans? Does your family know and understand this plan?

9. Give your kitchen a final glance. Is there anything else you think needs changing?

Dining Room

This room should be a little easier than the last. Only a few considerations here. Write out your answers as you consider the place where you gather at the table.

1. How would you rate this room on the organizational scale, with 10 being functional, logical, and relatively tidy, and 1 being utter chaos and clutter?

2. Do you have ample seating for your family? If not, what can you do to free up some space? Eat buffet style? Use TV trays? Some families simply don't have enough space for everyone to eat together. For many years we crammed four of us around a small table and parked the baby in the high chair. When he was out of the high chair and into a booster, we couldn't all fit around our table. Until we moved to a bigger house, we had to be creative. Kenzie and Mitch spent many nights eating picnic style on a blanket in the living room while Mom, Dad, and Spencer sat at the table. How is your seating space?

3. Other than eating, what else do you do in the dining room? Do you pay bills, play board games, or scrapbook?

Where do you store the items needed to do these tasks? Is there a nearby drawer where you could place the needed components? What about using a portable file box to stash your bills, calculator, stamps, and envelopes?

4. Is there anything else causing you confusion in this room? How are the walls? Are they littered with knickknacks? Are there other horizontal spaces causing you concern such as a desk, buffet, or table that is a catchall for clutter?

Bathroom

The bathroom can also be a source of many family squabbles. "He left the seat up!" "She left hair in the sink!" "Hey, who squeezed the toothpaste the wrong way?" Let's talk through this high-traffic room. Remember, if you have more than one bathroom, you'll need to repeat this exercise in a notebook or on a separate sheet of paper.

1. How would you rate this room on the organizational scale, with 10 being functional, logical, and relatively tidy, and 1 being utter chaos and clutter?

2. Open your cabinets and take a good look. How does the current setup rate as far as user-friendliness goes? Do you have the items most needed within closest reach? Are the items that are needed only occasionally in a spot further up or down in the cabinets?

3. What about your soaps, shampoos, toothpaste, towels, and washcloths? Are they being housed where they are easily accessible?

4. If space is limited, what can you do to create more? Can you install a shelf or add a basket or two in which to stash stuff?

5. Now, let's talk about the actual tub or shower. Is it a mess? Can you purchase an over-the-showerhead organizer to hold your bottles, shavers, and such?

Master Bedroom

I've heard it said many times that the master bedroom should be the room we put the most effort into making soothing, inviting, lovely, and clutter free. However, in reality many a master bedroom ends up looking more like a small flea market or junk yard—piles of paper strewn about; washed, yet still unfolded, clothing; projects half finished; bed unmade. Let's tackle this important room now.

1. How would you rate this room on the organizational scale, with 10 being functional, logical, and relatively tidy, and 1 being utter chaos and clutter?

2. For starters, as you look at your master bedroom, what are some changes that must be made to make it an inviting room?

3. If there are items that end up in this room because they have nowhere else to go, think through what other locations you can move them to. List those.

4. Is there anything aesthetically that needs to be done to the room so it can be more of a love nest than a

catchall? If so, what? Fresh paint? A new comforter or bedspread? Some enclosed storage like an armoire to hide some of the room's contents? Make a plan to look into any of these items. Be sure to check local papers to see what used items are for sale. We found three roll-top desks, an armoire, and many other beautiful pieces for pennies on the dollar through our local newspaper's classified section.

5. Are there ways you can make your bedroom reflect your marriage and the commitment you and your husband made? In our bedroom we have our framed wedding certificate, our wedding photo, and a beautiful sign my friend Trish painted that simply says, "June 21, 1986: 221 guests." When Todd and I see these visual reminders, we think of the 220 people we spoke our vows before (the 221st person was God) and purpose to do what we said we'd do—'til death do us part. We also hung a simple oval mirror in this grouping. When we face frustration in our marriage, as all couples do, the mirror causes each of us to keep the focus on our own self and what *we* are doing or not doing to make the marriage work. We are reminded of this when we spy our own reflection. What creative ways can your bedroom décor reflect your commitment?

Other Bedrooms

For each bedroom in your house (and the nursery, if you have one) you'll want to answer the following questions:

1. How would you rate this room on the organizational scale, with 10 being functional, logical, and relatively tidy, and 1 being utter chaos and clutter?

2. What obvious hot spots do you see that are causing disorganization to develop? Too many toys, papers, stuffed animals, etc.? What items need to be weeded out?

3. How and where will you store the following: current clothing, off-season clothing, toys (Do they belong in here or should they be in the basement or toy room?), school papers, books, etc.? Strategize for each room just where the most logical and user-friendly place is to put these things.

4. Are there any items that need to be put into storage for your kids to have when they're grown? No sense keeping these no-longer-used items in their rooms. Don't pitch them. Put them into their Nostalgia boxes and stash them away for the day when your children leave home and take all their junk…er… treasures…with them.

Office/Den

If you are fortunate enough to have space in your home to set up an office or study/den, make this space work for you. At the same time, fight the tendency to make such a room a magnet for wandering junk. To keep this from happening, quiz yourself on these points:

1. How would you rate this room on the organizational scale, with 10 being functional, logical, and relatively tidy, and 1 being utter chaos and clutter?

2. What daily and weekly functions take place in this room? Bill paying? Letter writing? Computer work, such as sending e-mails or surfing the Internet? A home business? A hobby such as scrapbooking or crafts? List what activities most frequently happen here and what ones only occasionally.

3. Make sure the room is set up in a way that corresponds to what you just wrote. Whatever tasks are performed here most often should have the corresponding tools within easy reach. The hobbies and activities that take place every once in a while can have their components in traveling totes or stashed in a closet, cupboard, or bin. For years I faced frustration when it was time to pay bills. I had a small table to work on, but stamps, envelopes, and return-address labels were stashed in a drawer in a bedroom at the back of the house. Every time I needed a stamp, I had to trek to the back of the house to retrieve one. Because the table in my workspace had no drawers, I assumed it couldn't accommodate stamps and such. One day I happened upon a clever little organizer with slots designed for file folders. It took up residence on top of that old table and held the items I needed in order to pay those bills.

    List the most frequently performed tasks on down to the least and then check to see if the layout of your office corresponds properly.

4. Are there any purchases that might make this work-space more functional? Don't always assume you need to trek to an office supply store and pay full price. Check secondhand stores and dollar stores. They usually have items at great savings.

Storage

Now, how about those items that you don't use on a regular basis. How are they stacking up...literally? This is where you may just have to bite the bullet and invest in some quality bins. I used all my Christmas and birthday money one year to purchase twenty clear Rubbermaid bins for our storage area. Sure, I could have bought myself a new outfit or gotten a French manicure, but I have *never* regretted the day I bought these wonderful organizational pieces. I even picked out lids of different colors to help in the storing: red ones for Christmas decorations, green for other holiday items, blue for the kid's nostalgia items, etc. Best buy I ever made!

The bins worked great and since they are see-through, it's easy to locate needed items. Some women suggest numbering your boxes and then keeping a notebook or note cards that list what items are in each box. That might work for you too. Let's tackle your storage now.

1. How would you rate your storage plan on the organizational scale, with 10 being functional, logical, and relatively tidy, and 1 being utter chaos and clutter?

2. How are you currently handling items that need to be in storage? Is this working? Why or why not?

3. Take inventory of what you have insisted on keeping in storage thus far. Are all these items really necessary?

Be ruthless. Go through your storage and pitch what you really don't need to keep clinging to.

4. Once you have waded through the junk and kept out only the treasures, decide how and where you will store what remains. Will you keep it in the basement? garage? shed or outbuilding? What about the attic? Also look for unused space under stairwells and beds. Again, as with the office, make sure the items that are needed most are easily accessible.

Closets

Whether they are in a bedroom or the hallway, closets can be a major culprit behind creeping clutter. Attack them head-on! Don't be intimidated. Walk boldly before each closet in your dwelling, and ask yourself the following questions:

1. How would you rate this space on the organizational scale, with 10 being functional, logical, and relatively tidy, and 1 being utter chaos and clutter?

2. What items are being stored in here and why?

3. What items *should* be located here?

4. Are there ways the items can be subdivided once in this closet? (Hats, gloves, and mittens in smaller boxes? Card games in a small bin? Medical supplies in small plastic baskets or old shoeboxes?)

Garage

Yes, yes…I know what you're thinking! *This is a man's domain. I'm not touching this one.* He *needs to organize that scrap heap!* Hang on, ladies. Now I am certainly not against getting your hubby, if you have one, in on the act, but we are talking about moms getting organized, not dads. Let's brainstorm some ways you can help get this rubbish-attracting room under control. This is our last section. Write down your answers with a smile. We are almost through.

1. How would you rate this part of your home on the organizational scale, with 10 being functional, logical, and relatively tidy, and 1 being utter chaos and clutter?

2. Has this place been thoroughly dejunked or are there items here your family doesn't use? Rid this space of old bikes, balls and bats, roller blades, and ice skates that no longer fit. Again, which will it be—charity or garage sale? Keeping them around any longer isn't an option!

3. How will you rearrange the garage so that it's both parent- and kid-friendly? What items need to be within your reach? Your husband's? How about the kiddos' reach? How can you shuffle everyone's stuff to create a space that functions well for all involved?

4. Are there any purchases you need to make to better organize this area of your home (shelves, bins, peg boards, etc.)?

Whew! Just thinking through all this was exhausting—let alone your having to actually do it. If you have completed any important step, you are to be commended! It's no easy undertaking to break old habits and think out of the box when it comes to forming new ones. So congratulate yourself.

Time for a little reward. Maybe a hot cup of strong espresso or a cold glass of sweet tea? You've earned it! Take one of the treasured breaks that you dreamed about in chapter 2 once you have completed this dejunking and realigning process.

The Tidy (*Somewhat Tidy*) Toy Room

If you have a separate room, area, the basement, or family room in which you keep the children's toys, consider implementing some of the following ideas to help with the tidiness.

Utilize baskets, boxes, and bins. This is a way to store toys where they are but keep the clutter they cause at a minimum. Ever since our kids were little, we've taught them munchkin microorganizing. That is just my fancy term for taking an area that could be overrun with chaos and breaking it down into manageable, bite-size, kid-friendly chunks. Our daughter, when small, had a few bins for her dollies and their clothes and accessories. Mitchell had an old fishing-tackle box to organize his leather-working supplies given to him by Grandma. It held pieces of leather, tools, snaps, and grommets perfectly. Spencer has always had "guy boxes" to keep his action figures in. These are plastic file boxes from the department store meant to hold hanging files. They are the perfect size to hold the "guys" and their various components. They are portable with their built-in handles, and they stack well. We organized them by sticking labels on the fronts noting what items were supposed to be in them or by sorting by the boxes' colors. *Star Wars* guys were in the blue box; *Lord of the Rings* characters in the black box, and so forth.

Search for free storage stuff. Many department, drug, and grocery stores occasionally get rid of display racks. We have gotten several wonderful display-stacking bins, clear plastic baskets, and even rolling metal displays that have helped us organize the kids' belongings in the toy area and the garage. Simply give your name and phone number to a store manager, and ask him if he would give you a quick call before discarding anything. Or occasionally inquire about any such display racks when you are in their store.

Combine fun and function. Store dolls and stuffed animals in a cute foot locker. Put small toys in various-size hat boxes that have been covered with self-adhesive paper. Look for fun colors and styles that would fit well in a toy room.

Craft it with crates. Use several inexpensive colored crates, stacked on their sides, to create an organizational wall. Designate different crates for different toys. Use some for art and craft supplies. Use smaller plastic baskets and shoebox-size boxes to further organize smaller items that are likely to get lost, for example: colored pencils, crayons, stickers, and safety scissors.

What Works for Me

Contributed by Laura Wittmann, British Columbia

As a mom with kids in a traditional school, I keep their backpacks organized and ready to go at a "backpack station" by my front door. I have a little nook right next to the front hall closet that works perfectly for this.

The kids know where to deposit their backpacks when they come home from school because each of them has a designated hook. Backpacks are up off the floor and kept from being a tripping hazard. They are left at the station at all times. I also have wicker baskets underneath the backpacks for notes for me or other things that need to be put away after I see them first.

In the evenings the kids ensure they have everything they

need for the next day packed into their backpacks and ready to go, which means no searching endlessly in the mornings for anything. This is a huge timesaver for us and also empowers our children by giving them clear boundaries and expectations.

What Works for Me

Contributed by Marybeth Whalen, North Carolina

My favorite tips for organizing my home and homeschool:

- *Take captive every moment.* Learn to multitask if you haven't already. Clean out your car while your gas is pumping, unload a load of dishes while your beginning reader sounds out words aloud at the kitchen table.

- *Have a designated homeschool area* for books, papers, notebooks, art supplies, school supplies, etc. This doesn't need to be a whole room. We have devoted a corner of our laundry room.

- *Use assignment books to record daily assignments, chores/ responsibilities, and activities for that day.* Kids like knowing what to expect each day, and this way the accountability is placed on them.

- *Train kids to do chores.* Designate a time to train them (summer or Christmas break is good).

- *Have a basket to corral all library books.* Train kids to return books to this basket. Use your library's online catalog to place holds, check on due dates, and renew books.

- *Ask "What would make my life easier?"* Ask for gift cards for Christmas and birthday. Purchase something that would help you: electric pencil sharpener, new bookshelf, large basket for books, containers.

5

COMBATING
OVERCOMMITMENT

● ●

Let's face it. The real reason most of us moms have trouble with time management is that our plates are so full with outside commitments that God and our families get the leftovers. And most times, the leftovers are tiny scraps, minuscule morsels that aren't worth tossing to the family pet. But somehow we mistakenly surmise that our families can survive on a steady diet of them. And God? Well, certainly he sees how busy we are. He must understand why we can't carve out time to connect with him.

Our society applauds busyness. It breathes busyness. It even scolds those who have the audacity to slow their lives down and drop some of their commitments at schools, community centers, and churches. The exception we make is when such a person is diagnosed with a serious illness or loses a loved one. Then we understand. We might even politely excuse that person from the rat race—at least for a month or so.

Success in our culture used to be measured by what neighborhood you lived in or what kind of car your family drove. Do you know how society gauges success now? By how busy you are. Sitting in the bleachers at a Little League game, what do you hear?

Mom #1: "Oh, Lisa! Good to see you. How *are* you?"

Mom #2: "Oh, busy! So busy…with Sarah in both tap and ballet, and Jason playing baseball and spring soccer, too, we're on the go every night of the week. You should see the calendar on our fridge! Not a blank square any day this month. Yep, we are busy, busy, busy."

Now what will be mom #1's natural tendency after hearing that monologue? Right! She'll want to one-up mom #2. She'll have to give a long rundown of just how swamped her family schedule is as well. She wouldn't ever want to think her own kids weren't participating in the sports and activities that other kiddos were excelling at. No siree…she'll want to paint her own dear family in the same bold shade of busy.

I've often wondered what the scene in the bleachers would be like if one brave woman, when the busy buzz began and it was her turn to speak, were courageous enough to step up to the plate and say:

Oh, our family has been very intentional lately about slowing down our hectic life. In fact, we just dropped dance lessons. Neither girl showed any real talent in the area, and they'd each already had a year of lessons. That was enough for them to learn to appreciate the arts. We also told all three kids they could participate in one sport per year, so they each had to pick their favorite. Ryan chose baseball, so we are having fun as a family watching him this season. I also resigned from all my responsibilities at church, except the one I really love—teaching a Bible study in the local nursing home. And I stepped down as head of the PTA. I'll still attend the meetings, of course, but someone else can take a turn at leading.

It has been so wonderful to spend more time together as a family. We made homemade pizzas last night and got out the home videos of the kids when they were young. My, how time flies! Can't believe how quickly they've grown and how soon they'll be gone from our home. Makes us really treasure the short season we have left. We love having time together and being at home first rather than constantly dashing from one frenzied activity to the next. As a result, I'm more easily able to keep the house picked up and have a nutritious hot meal on the table each night. And once the kids are in bed, Joe and I snuggle up and share a cup of coffee together and take time for just the two of us.

Oh, please! This woman would be instantly run out of town. Tarred and feathered, no less. Does anyone have the nerve to actually live that way? I mean, what about all the programs and committees? They aren't going to run themselves. Each woman needs to do her fair share. Pull her own weight. And those poor kids. Being limited in their activities. They'll probably end up on Dr. Phil's couch.

Truth be told, there's something in us that wants to paint those who choose a less busy lifestyle than we do as uncommitted. They're slackers, those families who don't put in the time and effort the rest of us are putting in. How dare they!

But deep down in our hearts, we are actually envious. We secretly wish we had the courage to jump off the activity merry-go-round, but the truth is, it's spinning so fast that if we jump now, we're sure to get hurt. It's less painful to just keep riding and spinning. At least it's familiar.

Bring Back Mayberry

My daughter and her friends have gotten me hooked on something I never dreamed I'd like. It's not the latest junk-food craze or a fashion fad that has burst upon the teenage scene. Nope. It's something that has been around for years, and I could have easily discovered it for myself, but I never did. It wasn't until this group of girls began riding around in our minivan to games and classes during the week that my addiction began. Yep, blame this one on Kenzie, Kim, and Traci. I am as big a fan of this activity as those three girls are, and I'm not even ashamed to admit it to you.

I love country music!

It's out in the open now. (Guess I can start rolling down my windows as I drive.) I love the way many of these songs tell tear-jerking stories and paint vivid pictures of American life. One of my favorite songs is by the group Rascal Flatts from their album *Melt*. When I first heard it on the radio, I wanted to holler out loud "That's it!" because it so perfectly echoed my sentiments. The title is "Mayberry." When I hear the lead singer reminiscing about sitting on a porch and sipping a Cherry Coke and treating Sunday as a time to rest rather than striving for progress as he laments how he misses Mayberry, I want to roll down the windows and shout a hearty amen!

How I love the picture painted in that song! I have often thought about this concept with my own past woven in. I miss pickup games of neighborhood kickball and making up dance recitals on our front porch, charging admission to the other kids on the block. I miss Kool-Aid stands, my brother and me sneaking dark, sweet cherries my mom put up each summer from the garage freezer, and endless games of frozen tag. I miss kids just being kids.

Today's youth are hurried. They don't play ball games unless there is a head coach, a whistle-toting referee, and an official team roster. Our free time is severely scheduled away—activities, lessons, commitments. Even summers are full of camps and contests, leaving little hanging-around time for going down to the fishin' hole. Most kids today don't even know what a fishin' hole is! It's a sad fact—our days are chock-full of endless activities that rob us of down time and any meaningful family time. Even current TV commercials accurately assert that families today have lost the habit of enjoying a meal together. Enough already! I say we curb the activities and bring back the family table!

Swimming Against the Tide

Carla was a mom with a middle-school-age son. He played on the local homeschool basketball team. Everyone, it seemed, had their boys on the team, so when Jason asked his parents if he could join, they said yes.

Jason attended the practices. He learned the basics of the game, and then the regular season began. Because it was a homeschool league, many of the away games meant traveling 30 or more miles to take on an opponent. Carla, her husband, and their other five children made the trek to watch each of Jason's basketball match-ups. This often took several hours out of those days.

One night, when Jason's squad was playing a team from a town about an hour away, a winter storm hit. Carla's family was already on their way to the game and made it to the gymnasium safe and sound, but after the game they faced a ride home that would be twice as long due to the horrible road conditions. Halfway home, while slipping and sliding over the ice-covered highway, Carla began thinking:

> What are we doing? I don't know if we'd venture out on a night like this to help my elderly mother-in-law if she needed us to come over, but we'll haul the entire family out to watch a basketball game. I wonder if Jason even likes playing basketball. Actually, he isn't very gifted when it comes to this sport. Most nights he doesn't even get in the game, unless of course we're way ahead of the opposing team. So we all come watch him watch his team, paying almost ten bucks each time for our family to get in, and there are over twenty games scheduled this winter! Not to mention the gasoline it takes to get to the game. And what about the time involved? Jason spends nearly ten hours a week on this activity alone. Is this really worth it?

Thankfully, Carla's family made it home safely that night. But they decided to reevaluate the situation. They sat down with Jason and discussed his involvement in basketball. Turns out he had only joined because of that old adage, "Everyone else is doing it!" He recognized he wasn't a gifted ball handler and he wasn't so great on defense. He most likely wouldn't earn a spot on the starting lineup. And he admitted that basketball was not a sport he was enthused about playing. What he really wanted to spend his time doing was playing music on his guitar and singing, things he was already showing talents in. And he was interested in becoming an amateur filmmaker in his spare time. When Jason and his parents looked objectively at the current basketball situation, factoring in the time and money it was costing their family each week, they decided it wasn't worth it.

Jason dropped off the team. Shock! Instead of being chided for his lack of persistence, he is to be commended. He and his family made the tough call and did what was right for their household. And today Jason is a young adult serving on the mission field, assisting other missionaries in the area of media, music, and filmmaking. He didn't suffer harm for his decision to drop off the team.

Now, please don't get me wrong. I am not saying it's a bad thing to have a son on a basketball team. Our older son plays for that very same team today. What I am saying is, "*Why* are your kids on the team or in the show or on the stage?" Sports and activities can be wonderful for children and teens. They help them learn teamwork, master a skill, and exercise mind and body. I'm not even one who believes that if your child does not land the lead or earn a spot on the starting lineup he should throw in the towel. Some kids love certain sports enough that simply being a member of the team thrills them. Besides, we have always told our kids that sometimes more is learned by sitting on the bench than stealing the show.

What I am urging you to do is to look at *why* you and your children are involved in the activities you are. Don't sign up for soccer just because it's soccer season. Don't try out for the play just because everyone else is. Counsel your kids to choose sports and activities they really enjoy or are gifted at.

Scaling Back

Here's an example of how we handle outside interests at our house. Our kids can choose one sport per year to be involved in. Kenzie chose volleyball. Mitchell and Spencer both are baseball freaks, so when Little League sign-up happens in our city each spring, they are all over it.

Mitchell is old enough to play for the Warriors for Christ home-school basketball team in our county. Two years ago he announced he wanted to play this sport too. Todd and I told him we'd think about it and get back to him. It would have been easy for us to hold fast to our "one sport per kid" rule. We decided, however, that basketball in the winter would be a good fit for our family for a number of reasons.

First, it would keep him physically active. We noticed a tendency for all of us—except our winter-sports and volleyball-playing daughter—to pork-up a little over the winter months. The sweating, stretching, and shooting would be good exercise. It also kept him on task with his schoolwork. When faced with an open-ended day, he tended to lolly-gag when it came to getting his school assignments done. However, on the days when he had a practice or game, it served as incentive for him. He wanted to plug away at his schoolwork, often starting early and finishing by lunch, so he could get ready for his game.

Playing basketball in the winter also works for us as parents in another way. If we encounter any bad behavior or bad attitudes from our son, the practice or game is off. We are blessed to have a coaching staff in our league that is on the same page as the parents. They encourage us to "bust" our boys and forbid them to come to the game if they don't keep up their schoolwork or misbehave. With Mitchell, it only happened once. That was all it took for him to see that we meant business.

Because allowing Mitchell to play two sports per year bends our "one sport per year" rule, we have him pay for it. You heard me right. It costs $120 to play a second sport, and he has to fork over the money himself. He watches the neighbor's dog, does yard work for Grandpa, and anything else he can to earn every penny that is due.

Insisting that our kids pay for a second sport makes them really think through whether this is something they greatly desire or if they're just signing up because all their friends are.

The Too-Full Platter

Our children aren't the only ones who fill their time with outside activities. Sometimes we moms can be the main offenders! I know how tempting it can be to overfill our plates. When presented with another out-of-the-home opportunity, we glance at our platter. Certainly we don't think about removing anything before placing something else on it. We are certain that if we just rearrange things a little, we can somehow make it all fit. Moms today have plates so full of outside commitments that even the strongest plate Chinette makes won't hold it, no matter what their commercials claim. But does this have to be so?

We are all given twenty-four hours in a day to do what we must and what we wish. The trouble is that many of us confuse those two categories. We mistake the "must do's" for the "want to's." When feeling overwhelmed by all the tasks we think we *must* do, we need to realize that many of them are *choices* we have made. We can clear them off our schedules...if we dare. But we are so in step with the rat race and have so many people who are counting on us to continue running at this rapid pace that we feel trapped, victims of our own poor choices. What's a mom to do?

Face it, ladies, many of us take on too many outside roles at the expense of our families. This is a gut-wrenching topic for me because I am the *former* queen of overcommitment. (I have since been willingly dethroned; however, I do admit that at times I'm tempted to grab the crown and reclaim my reign.)

Beginning with my junior-high days, I discovered I could keep so busy with school and church commitments that it would distract me from the fact that my home was empty because my mother, a single mom, had to work outside the home to make ends meet. In addition, I discovered that by being in endless activities, I could appear to the outside world to really be someone.

I carried this into my early marriage. It actually seemed like a good thing for a while. My husband was on staff at a church, and since we didn't have kids for the first five years of our marriage, I could work and serve at the church and at the high school where I was a substitute teacher and cheerleading coach. Committee chairs and project heads loved me. They knew they could count on a "yes" rolling easily off of my lips when asked to help or even to take charge. In no time flat I had my days so packed with activities that I barely had time to breathe. As my husband has often warned me, "If you don't fill your time, a dozen people are out there waiting to fill it for you. Make sure you fill it up with the important rather than the trivial."

When he'd say this, I'd smile and think, *What a philosopher I married. He thinks too much!* Besides, I'd always figured him to be a low-capacity specialist who requires lots of alone time. He is energized by puttering and pondering and having lots of time to contemplate. (*Yawn!*) I, on the other hand, am a high-capacity idea person who craves brainstorming and collaborating and am most energized by being with people. (*Yeah!*) I'd listen to his "Take it slow, Karen" advice. And then I'd turn right around and say yes to something else.

And then we had a baby.

I took an entire two weeks off to recover from my emergency C-section and then laced my sneakers back up and tried to keep running. Little Mackenzie nearly flew out of her baby sling as I took her along for the ride. Life hit me smack between the eyes. I was forced to slow down and take inventory of my activity level.

You see, I was not prepared for the sweet, dark-haired, colicky baby who joined our family. She was high-need and fussy and wouldn't take a bottle, even one full of breast milk. Being a first-time, inexperienced mom, I never let my baby so much as whimper. I felt a crying baby was a sign of a bad mother. So I held her constantly and let her call all the shots for my schedule. She sure cramped my busy lifestyle.

What ensued in the next half a decade was a severe identity crisis. My identity was rooted in what I did or how I performed, not in my position in Christ. I cared far more about who others thought I was rather than who God was calling me to be. Because my measuring stick was all wrong, I felt like a failure. I was known by proxy—the youth pastor's wife or so-and-so's mom. My days were spent performing the hidden chores of homemaking and carrying out my mothering responsibilities. Even though I treasured my family, I also silently resented them, feeling my life as an at-home mom was keeping me from fulfilling my dreams and doing what I enjoyed. Worst of all, it kept me cooped up at home. It even prevented me from doing "ministry," or so I thought.

During that hidden period of my life God taught me that true service begins first with my family. I had to learn that God is much more concerned with the way I treat the members of my clan and my attitude within my four walls than he is with any outside service. I will be held more accountable for the way I run my home than how well the Mother–Daughter Banquet went off at church.

I also discovered that often my motives were wrong. I wanted to engage in activities, not because I felt *called* to do them, but because I felt *compelled* to do them so others would like me. This set up an unhealthy pattern. I spun my wheels and filled my days to get approval and attention, letting my family members fend for themselves.

At-home moms are especially prone to this pattern. Because we fear others will assume we have lots of time on our hands since we don't work outside the home, we prepare a five-course meal for someone who just had a baby, while our own family gets peanut-butter sandwiches and leftover macaroni and cheese. We spend time planning and teaching a wonderful Sunday school lesson while never intentionally training our own children in the things of God. We say, "Yes! Yes! Yes!" to outside commitments that come our way, while our families get "Maybe later." After all, we want to make sure we are pulling our weight at church or in the community.

I had to majorly scrape my too full plate off a few years ago due to some health issues. Then I made an effort to only place back on the plate those commitments I felt were God's directives for me. It was hard but so freeing! Did everyone understand? Of course not. But I need to please God and my husband with my time choices first.

I won't say my plate *never* gets too full these days. It does, but much less frequently than it used to. And now, because I'm more consistently keeping my schedule trimmed back, I recognize more easily when my platter is getting too heavy from the responsibilities that are there. I also set aside time each summer to reevaluate my life and ask God, my husband, Todd, and my kids if there is anything they think should go.

My friend Marielle recently moved from Michigan to Georgia. She is a high-capacity, busy mom and probably the smartest person I know. Before she moved, she was the homeschooling mom of three, worked part-time at her church as a children's director, held another weekend, part-time phone job, did foster care in her home, and was active in her circle of friends. I expected her first call to me in Michigan to be one of sadness since she had left so many people and activities behind.

When she did call, I was shocked by what I heard her say. Her family was starting to settle in to their new place. Her husband liked his new job. However, they hadn't made any connections yet with new families or found a new church home. And guess what? They loved it!

As I asked her what they had been up to over the course of those last few weeks, she relayed tales of helping the kids do their schoolwork without a phone ringing, of unhurried afternoons exploring downtown Atlanta, of enjoying leisurely, home-cooked dinners as a family with no one having to dash off anywhere at night. It took moving to a new state for her to realize how overcommitted she had been and what wonderful times she'd been missing with her loved ones.

Although I had intentionally scraped off my own plate in the three years before this phone call came, it made me stop and think about what commitments I was holding on to that I should let go of. It also made me wonder how many moms would probably be envious of my friend. She could easily bow out of all her responsibilities and commitments since she was moving away. Perhaps that's what it will take for some of us.

An Honest Look

I want to help you take a penetrating, honest look at what you say your priorities are and see if it matches the way you spend your time. Then you can weed out the activities you are not "called" to do. Sometimes seeing in black and white just what our choices look like helps us adjust and realign. First of all, list *in order* how your top-ten priorities line up. Don't get too specific. Use general categories. My example looks like this:

1. God
2. Husband
3. Children
4. Home responsibilities, including homeschooling
5. Extended family members
6. Close friends
7. Speaking and writing ministry responsibilities
8. Other friends, neighbors, and acquaintances
9. Volunteer activities outside my home
10. Hobbies and interests

Your turn! List your priorities. Oh...and please use a pencil.

1.
2.
3.
4.
5.
6.
7.
8.
9.
10.

Next, envision a typical week at your house. I know it will vary generally from week to week and season to season, but let's try to come up with what an average week right now looks like for you as far as time is concerned. Write out the time commitments you cannot change. Don't put in tasks you can perform at various times, just note the set appointments, meetings, practices, lessons, and so forth. Also, if you work outside the home, put that down too. Draw a downward line with an arrow through all the time slots each commitment takes. If there is a place your children must be, and you must stay there and wait for them, draw a line through the entire time. If you drop them off and return later to pick them up, just draw the line through your actual driving time. Again, do this in pencil, please.

	Monday	Tuesday	Wednesday
A.M. 6			
7			
8			
9			
10			
11			
Noon			
P.M. 1			
2			
3			
4			
5			
6			
7			
8			
9			
10			
11			
12			

Thursday	Friday	Saturday	Sunday

Next, list other seasonal responsibilities you have said yes to: committees, coaching assignments, church activities, civic and community responsibilities, scouting. Maybe you don't have a set time that you perform these activities each week, but sometime during the month or season you must spend time following through on the tasks you agreed to do. Next to them list the approximate time each responsibility requires of you, whether it's monthly or a one-time shot. Be realistic. Don't fool yourself by thinking you can pull off the entire Christmas pageant—casting, directing, finding costumes, building the set—in a total of three or four hours. Tell the truth about the time it takes for your responsibilities. Ready? Start writing. (If you are an extremely overcommitted gal, you may need more space than provided.)

Now, how about the kiddos? For your children, list their monthly and seasonal commitments along with the estimated amount of time each one requires per month or per activity. Again, be sensible in your estimation.

Now, before going any further, take a good, hard, honest look at your weekly schedule and the two other lists. Look at where you're spending your time and to what and to whom you are devoting those precious hours. Then glance back to the section where you listed what you say your top-ten priorities are. How do they match up? Are you allowing your #5 or #7 or even #10 priority to take precedence over a #1, #2, or #3? Do you put off time with a higher priority while devoting lots of time to lesser priorities?

The first time I did this exercise, I was shocked! While I *said* my kids came far before my close friends and acquaintances on my list (they were my #3, my friends, #6), the truth appeared to be exactly the opposite. I was allowing unlimited phone calls to interrupt my schedule at all times of the day—while I held the little ones at bay or put their needs and wishes off...sometimes until the next day.

I'd heard some rumbles of complaint from my kids: "Mom, you are always talking to Mrs. So-and-So on the phone!" But I reasoned they simply were not ministry minded. Didn't they see Mrs. So-and-So needed me right then? If I didn't talk to her, who would?

It took some medical conditions and stress-related symptoms that wouldn't go away for me to realize I was taking on way too many outside issues and crises in my life that really were not meant for me to handle. Because I was addicted to getting the approval of others, I had become a dumping ground for people. They needed to talk; they needed their kids watched; they needed me to look up a phone number for them; they called with their crises...and suddenly they became mine. All because I did one simple thing: I picked up the phone.

Hello! Can anyone say "caller ID"? We finally got that blessed service added to our monthly phone bill. Oftentimes I would answer the phone, thinking it was going to be my mother, from whom I was expecting a call. Instead, it was another person desiring my time. Screening our calls made it possible to take the ones we needed to and return the others later at a more convenient time.

Now, I don't fault these people. The situation was actually *my* fault.

I'd welcomed their phones calls, never letting on that I was busy at the moment. Because I let others call me at all hours of the day, interrupting my time with my kids and their schoolwork or my family's attempt to enjoy a hearty round of Kings in the Corner, I set up an unhealthy pattern. Others knew I was a "drop whatever I am doing gal" who would come to their rescue. However, for the sake of my health and my family's sanity, it had to stop. And I wondered, too, how often my availability prevented these women from running to God, the one they should have headed to in the first place.

Other women have been wonderful models for me in this area. I think of Kelly, my best friend from college. She homeschools her three youngest kids, and she takes that task very seriously. I know better than to call her between nine o'clock and noon. This is when she has her most intense, formal schooling time. She treats it just like a job. She and the kids trek downstairs to their schoolroom and don't emerge until it's time for lunch.

Kelly has caller ID and regularly screens her calls. I never felt slighted when she didn't pick up and then called me later in the afternoon to see what I wanted. But somehow I had a hard time doing that to those who called me. I was afraid they'd get mad at me for ignoring their calls. Now that I have made the switch and no longer have a "phone ministry," as my husband used to half-jokingly and half-seriously tease, I have much more time with my family. And to my surprise, I didn't lose friends over it. I have just had to readjust how I connect with them.

Except for three of my closest friends, who all live far away, I don't sit and chat on the phone with people like I used to. I'd rather set a time every few months for outings with friends.

Pleasing God or Pleasing People?

If you take seriously the notion of purging your schedule of unnecessary commitments and activities, there will be people who simply don't understand. They will question and scowl. They will utter guilt-inducing phrases such as, "Gee, it must be nice." They will attempt to make you feel guilty or subtly assert that you aren't somehow committed or faithful to the cause or even to the Lord.

I have met dear, dear women who are totally tired and burned out. They are guilty of overserving, especially in their churches. They decide to let others set their agendas, and they mistakenly and foolishly believe that involvement in church activities equals commitment to God. It's sad, but true: One can be maxed out with Christian activities and church committees and have no time for God. No time for having a personal relationship with him, getting to know him by spending time reading his Word and connecting with him through prayer. They are busy *serving* God, yet they simply don't have time for the God whom they serve.

Sometimes we fear our absence at church activities speaks volumes about our commitment, so we make sure we never miss. I'm not talking about the main Sunday service. I'm talking about filling our weeks with endless meetings and activities while neglecting our home responsibilities. Sometimes we sign up to serve in order to fill the void we feel because our relationship with God is at a standstill. Sometimes we simply need to stand still, apart from these spiritual activities, to rekindle our spiritual fires.

While reading through the New Testament, I am often envious of the first-century Christians. I read nothing about church bazaar committee chairs, Bible-school craft leaders, quiz-team teachers, and Ladies' Aid Societies. While all these activities are well and good, when we feel we must have some part in them all, we miss the point entirely.

God's Word paints a picture of the church by using the illustration of the body. We all play a part—like a nose, mouth, or foot. No part is more important; all parts are equal. While some are more visible, all are necessary. The illustration is speaking directly about spiritual gifts in the church, such as teaching and administration. But I think we can find application when we think of the programs and projects that are part of the modern church. For some of us, instead of recognizing the church as one body made up of many parts, we have been trying to play all the parts in our attempts to fit into the church body.

Please don't feel that if you placed God in the #1 slot on your priority list that it means all church activities belong there too. In fact, when we place anything other than God in our God slot, we wind up, instead, with a god (little *g*). What we have is an idol. You needn't look far in the Bible to see what God thinks of idols. We are told to have nothing to do with them!

What's Got to Go

Now, back to our little assignment. For starters, is there anything you or your offspring are committed to that should be crossed off your list? Come on, you know in your gut the things you've said yes to that you shouldn't have. When asked to take on a commitment or responsibility, we need to really ask ourselves, "Am I called to do this?" instead of what we moms often ask ourselves, "Am I capable?"

Bad question. Moms are *more* than capable. We have what I call the "curse of capability." When our capability is our plumb line, we take on way too much. *Stop!* When asked about volunteering, don't answer right away. Take time to pray and consult your husband. Determine if you are really called for an activity. And remember: If you aren't called and you say yes to the task anyway, you are taking the joy away from the person whom God did call to do the job. Don't be a joy stealer! Remind yourself often that every need is not necessarily your call.

Also strive to become keenly aware of the activities you are allowing your kids to be a part of that are unnecessary—those time-wasters that are robbing them of a true childhood. Don't allow your kids to become overscheduled, stressed out, and sports overloaded. Make it possible for them to experience carefree days of imaginary play or exploits like building a fort or clubhouse. Take a thorough look at that list you made. Can anything go? If so, highlight it.

Now, if an activity is something you already committed to, then by all means see that commitment through. But get out of that responsibility at the first possible moment if you feel it's not something you are supposed to be doing.

And don't forget to talk through this exercise with your husband. Seek his advice. Often husbands can spot the stresses in our lives better than we can. Has this little assignment made you think, *Well…what about my husband? He is the one who should be doing this little inventory. That man has said yes to too many responsibilities at church/school/work/ wherever. He plays sports with his friends way too often. And he watches the pros on television play even more often. He is the one who should change!* If that runs through your mind, I am not going to counsel you in either extreme. I will not suggest you let him have it, pointing out his faults in this area and demanding that he clear his schedule immediately. Nor will I tell you to just zip your lip and pray, letting God deal directly with him (although some of you may be feeling that a quick lightning bolt might shake him up a bit and get his attention).

No, the most appropriate path is somewhere down the middle. While whining and nagging gets a wife nowhere but a permanent spot in the "Bossy Wives Hall of Fame," I see nothing wrong with calmly and honestly sharing your feelings and concerns in a nonaccusatory way. Let your man know how you see his decisions and time commitments affecting you and the kids. Make sure he knows you are on the same team, that you want what is best for him and your family in the long run. Then leave the decision up to him. Try, within reason, to adjust to his choices. In the meantime you can still pray that God will change his heart, if it needs changing. Sometimes, however, it's us who need to make the change.

Embracing Your Schedule

When I first became a mom, my husband was a youth pastor in a wonderful country church. Sundays were very full days for us: two services, Sunday school, evening youth group. Monday was Todd's day off, and our church was very respectful of this. Monday was Todd's "sabbath."

However, Tuesday through Friday he was one busy guy. He put in time at the office from 8:00 A.M. until 5:30 P.M. or so. Evenings found him at a meeting or activity, often until past ten o'clock. Saturday was a mixed bag. Usually it was catch-up day for him workwise, but we were sometimes able to do something fun as a family or take an extended shopping trip into the city. His schedule meshed pretty well with our family and friends', and for the most part we felt we were on a very typical American-family timetable. While weekdays found us on the go at night—meetings or church teenagers' sporting events—we simply brought the baby along, and it seemed to work fine.

However, when I was pregnant with our second child, Todd left full-time ministry. Our growing family demanded more time than he could devote to being a member of the clergy. He didn't want to end up like so many men we knew who were devoting dozens of hours trying to save everyone else's families while their own wives and children were starved for their attention, getting the leftovers of their time and very little of their energy.

For a while Todd worked for a friend who owned a furniture and appliance store. Then, when I was pregnant with our third child, our friend Phil referred Todd to work for General Motors. The wages were good, and the job meant full benefits. Rising to the top of 17,000 applicants, and after passing all the tests, Todd was hired. Yippee! I was elated! Until he came home and told me the shift he'd be on: second. No, not a typical factory second shift of 3:00 P.M. to 11:00 P.M. This one was from 5:30 P.M. to 2:00 A.M. Factoring in the 45-minute commute required, it meant Todd would be gone from around 4:30 each afternoon until nearly 3:00 in the morning, and he would need to shower and sleep 'til nearly noon. Then he'd get up and do it all over again, five, sometimes six, days a week.

Bummer.

Well, ladies...true to my often nagging and complaining nature, I began to grumble. "How am I supposed to keep these kids quiet until nearly noon each day? You won't ever get to have supper with us at night. I'll have to handle bedtime all by myself. And I'm such a light sleeper; my sleep will get interrupted every night when you return home. Besides, after six years of having babies, I *just* got everyone sleeping through the night. This setup stinks!"

I could not see the flowers, only the weeds. I failed to recognize that God had pulled strings to land my hubby a good-paying job with wonderful benefits! And having him home in the afternoons meant I could go to the doctor and dentist all alone. No more getting my teeth cleaned with a baby on my lap and one at my feet. And this setup worked beautifully when it came to homeschooling. Todd could give a spelling test or listen to a child read out loud while I tackled a more intense assignment with another child. I could even spend an hour every afternoon writing!

I needed to learn an important lesson: *We need to willingly accept the lifestyle that results from our husband's work schedule.* (Ouch! I know that hurt some of you like it hurt me the first time I heard it.)

Now, if your husband has a say in what shift he will work or what his starting and ending times will be at the office, talk about it together and find what works best for your family. But if he has no say in the matter, for crying out loud don't beat the poor guy up about this. It isn't his fault, and maybe, just maybe, God has something to teach you through this situation.

The Pleasures of Plate Scraping

Our goal in this chapter has been to take an objective look at our commitments and decide which ones should stay and which ones should go. I hope you'll make this a priority in the next few months. Plate scraping isn't easy, but the rewards are well worth the effort. Just think of all the important people in your life and the time you'll be able to devote to them instead of to another committee or crew. While there is certainly nothing wrong with volunteerism, and I firmly believe in being an involved member of a local church, we need to keep first things first. Don't let activity crowd out importance. My accountability partner, Mary Steinke, often asks me this probing question when I am contemplating a commitment: "Karen, is this for *activity* or *eternity?*" Another way to approach this is to ask, "Ten years from now, which one will I be more thankful I chose?" Both of these questions can help keep our priorities. Overall, seek to strike a balance that pleases your husband, is doable for you, and honoring to God.

In the area of overcommitment I have three quotes that help keep me pointed in the right direction. The first one I read in a book on time management nearly twenty years ago. I don't remember the book, and I don't recall the author. I just know the sentence leapt off the page and has been seared in my mind ever since (and it's printed on our checks so I can ponder it often):

"Beware of the barrenness of a busy life."

Are we inclined to think of the busy life as a barren one? Usually not. We reason that folks who are busy are important. That it's somehow exciting and glamorous to live existences packed with activity. But in reality, it's an empty bag. It's a shallow and vacant pursuit. Barren.

The second sentence that keeps me focused is one I have heard uttered since I was a young girl:

"If Satan can't make you bad, he'll make you busy."

How true. Most of us know better than to be "bad." But busy? Ah, we fall for that trick over and over again.

And finally, my friend Becky Glenn has for years taught a wonderful workshop for women on slowing down the pace of life. She challenges her audiences with this statement:

"Don't take on more than you can pray for."

Boy, the first time I heard her say that, did it ever hit me between the eyes! Before hearing it phrased that way, rarely did I ever consider that admonition. When a responsibility came along, I simply asked myself if it sounded like a fit or if I could somehow find the time. I didn't think to ponder, "Do I really feel called to this task, so called that I can take on the extra time it will take to pray adequately for

all the components it involves and for all the people I will be working alongside?" Putting it in terms like that really makes me take a
step back and seriously consider what I'm being asked to do *before*
answering.

My desire is that we will make it a habit to regularly take inventory and see where our lives fall on the busyness scale. That we'll
strike a healthy balance between activity and eternity, and we'll keep
that rubber spatula handy for the times we need to do a little plate
scraping.

Once our plates are squeaky clean, just how do we manage our
hours each day so we can properly attend to the priorities we have?
The next time we meet, we'll talk about time.

● ● ● ● ● ● ● ● **From the Heart of a Kid** ● ● ● ● ● ● ● ●

Overcommitment is something everyone deals with, even kids. I
know—big shock there! Many times kids don't even like the sport or
activity they're involved in; however, because a best friend is doing
it, or a cousin, or whoever, they feel the need to do it too. When
they hear their moms say, "No," it usually doesn't go over too well.
Am I right? Moms, I suggest giving kids the freedom of choosing
what they do but not *how many* things they do.

For instance, this tends to be a huge thing with sports. Unless your
children are extremely athletic and love every sport, they are probably only in sports for the social part, especially if you homeschool.
Tell them how many sports they can play, but let them choose the
sports. Sit down with them and help them decide what sport they
are best at, and encourage them to choose that one. If this activity
is a social thing, tell your children you'll take them to some of the
games so they can see their friends, but they don't have to play,
especially when they don't even enjoy it as much.

A good example of this would be that I love and play volleyball. I am fairly good at it, and I usually don't sit and watch the entire game from the bench; however, I couldn't make a basket if the hoop were the size of a barn and I was right over the top of it. Because my parents only allow me to choose one "free" sport and I must pay for any others, I stick to volleyball.

Now, what if your children aren't athletic, but when it comes to other things such as painting, drawing, writing, singing, piano—stuff like that—they are amazing? Maybe they still feel pressure from their peers to play sports even though they don't enjoy them. If that's your child, you can say to him or her, "You know, you are so good at painting, writing, singing, piano (whatever it is), and I think you have a lot of potential. If you want to sit out this sports season, we'll spend the time and money doing something you really enjoy and are gifted at instead." This will be a big relief to your son or daughter!

Above all else, it's true that kids want their parents' approval and encouragement. Whatever they do, tell them you are proud of them and their efforts. Be their biggest cheerleaders!

☺ Mackenzie

Confessions of a Prayer Wimp

Are you a woman who struggles to make time for prayer? I am. While I love to read my Bible, attend Bible studies, write encouraging notes to other Christians, and teach the things of God to my children, I seem to put spending time actually praying low on my list of priorities. Oh, don't get me wrong. I have a prayer list I use. I make sure my hubby, kids, and family members are prayed for. But spending large chunks of time connecting with God through serious prayer doesn't come easily for me. I get distracted. I get up to take care of something I forgot and then never return. And to top it off, comments about those who are "prayer warriors" seem to leave me feeling inadequate and unspiritual.

Although I'd like to think that being women of prayer should just come naturally to us, I know better. I have found that, like many other aspects of my life, I have to have a plan in order to make it happen. Here are some suggestions that have helped me to become more intentional in this important area of my life.

Set up space. This can be anywhere, even a corner in a room. My friend Lisa uses a walk-in closet as her "prayer closet." If having a permanent place is not an option, create a portable tote bag or basket filled with all the items you might need during a quiet time alone with God each day. You could include a Bible, journal, pretty pen, mug, bags of tea or flavored coffees, stationery, your church's directory, an address book, and a devotional or Christian book you're currently reading. Grab this when you find a slice of time in your day that you can spend focusing on growing your relationship with God.

If God brings someone to your mind, jot that person an encouraging note. This is why it's a good idea to have stamps, stationery or note cards, and addresses handy so you can get on this right away. You know good intentions get lost when we have to run around locating all the components needed to make them happen.

Have paper or a small notepad by your side. No, not to write down requests or what you sense the Lord is telling you. Those are great ideas too, but I use my paper in a different way. Although it doesn't sound very spiritual to admit, often when I am trying to pray, I am distracted by random thoughts that pop into my head: *I need to pick up eggs when we go to baseball tonight. I'd better drop by and pay the Internet provider bill. I think Lysa wanted me to send her that document by e-mail by tomorrow. I hope I don't forget!* When these thoughts interrupt my praying, I jot them down. That way I know I won't forget to take care of them later. And I don't hop up to take care of them then or wander off to find some paper only to get so sidetracked that my prayer time is over before it started!

Make a prayer notebook. A few years ago for Christmas I made my husband a prayer notebook. I purchased a desk-size, three-ring leather binder and placed paper and dividers in it so he could keep track of the requests he was praying for in a manner that made sense to him. In the front of the binder I put a laminated page with a Bible verse that is especially meaningful to him. Behind this, I placed one page from each member of our family. Author Emilie Barnes and I had spoken at an event together once where she told of tracing her grandchildren's hands and then using those papers to put her hands on as she prayed for them. I loved that concept, so we each traced our hands in a faint outline and then over it wrote five things we wanted Dad to pray for when he prayed for us. The boys wrote things like "That I will have a Christlike attitude when I play sports." Kenzie asked that he pray that she would love God more than the things of this world, that she would remain pure until her wedding day, and that her future husband would be rich ☺. Finally, we put a cropped picture of each of us on our individual pages, along with some scrapbooking decals. When having his time alone to pray, Todd turns to the pages of his family, places his hands over our "hands," and prays.

When keeping track of requests, spread them out over the course of the week. On Monday, pray for the missionaries you know abroad and here at home. On Tuesday, concentrate on extended family members. On Wednesday, workers, such as your pastor, church staff, Christian workers, and any writers or speakers you know who serve God. I find that I am more likely to have a consistent time praying each day when I have direction. Just sitting down to pray for everyone and everything in my life at once overwhelms me.

Take a hike! Getting out of the house and taking a walk can be a great time to focus your mind on those people and situations you want to remember in prayer.

Read the Good Book as well as a good book. While the Bible should be our main focus, any of the following books serve as great inspiration in this area. I like to reread at least one of these a year to keep me on the right track:

> *Praying God's Word* and *Believing God,* both by Beth Moore
>
> *Celebration of Discipline* by Richard Foster
>
> *What Happens When Women Pray* by Evelyn Christenson
>
> *What Happens When Women Say Yes to God* by Lysa TerKeurst
>
> Any of the books in "The Power of a Praying" series by Stormie Omartian

What Works for Me

Renee Wrage, Illinois

I desire to really get God's Word down inside my heart, so I have been faithfully memorizing Scripture for the past four years. As I read my Bible or hear a Scripture that really touches my heart, I write it down in a notebook. At the beginning of each month, I choose one of these verses to memorize, and I write it on a brightly colored index card (the ones that are all held together on a spiral wire). Each day while in the bathroom, I use the time to repeat the Scripture...over and over and over again! I only seem able to learn one Scripture a month, but that's twelve more than I knew last year at this time! And it's forty-eight more than I knew when I began this project four years ago!

6

TAKING CONTROL OF THE CLOCK

I was two weeks into motherhood. We had been showered with gifts and casseroles and well wishes. My mom had come to help clean the house and catch up on the laundry. She began her most important task—spoiling her first grandbaby. But now the time had come for me to reenter life and, the next morning, go back to church.

My friend Suzy and I were chatting on the phone that Saturday evening. Three months earlier she'd given birth to baby #3. She was an organized and devoted mom. I looked up to her as a mentor and took her advice seriously. Before hanging up the phone, I told her we planned on going to the 8:00 A.M. church service the next day just as we had done before we had Mackenzie. She ended our conversation by chuckling and saying, "Then you might want to build an extra hour or two into your morning routine now that you have a newborn so you won't be late to church."

I smiled when I hung up the phone. *Sweet Suzy. What a nice suggestion. Might even be necessary counsel for a woman who is unorganized.* This was one piece of advice I thought wasn't necessary for capable me. But, just for fun, I'd take it and when we were an hour *ahead* of schedule, we could stop off at The Wheel Inn for a lingering cup of coffee. Then I could tell Suzy how I took her advice but really hadn't needed it.

Yes, I built in that extra, unneeded, superfluous hour.

We arrived at church ten minutes late!

I never dreamed how much one little, seven-pound bundle could completely throw off my timing and ruin my schedule! When I stepped into the shower that morning, she awoke and was screaming to be fed. Since I was nursing, I had to step out of the shower and feed her. She was a slow eater, and it took her nearly 40 minutes. I had planned on discreetly doing this in a back booth at the restaurant under one of the cute blankets given to us by a knitting grandma at church. So much for *my* plans.

Once I was dressed, I picked my daughter up to finish burping her. Yep, you're one step ahead of me. Over my shoulder and down my back came all the contents of her little stomach, which didn't seem so little now. I had to completely change my clothes. Wait! I didn't have another outfit ironed. That cost me more precious time. The clock was ticking.

Once I was dressed again, I chose a cute outfit for Kenzie. Just as Todd went to get the car and I was buckling the baby into her car seat, she began to grimace. After a second or two of intense focusing, we heard the rumblings down south that spell (and smell) disaster. Oh well, I could change her in the church nursery. After all, it was a short drive to the church.

However, upon closer inspection, I discovered that not only had she blown out her diaper, but the blowout had shot up her back, into her hair, and out onto the car seat cover. I had to call Todd back into the house for reinforcement. He cleaned off the car seat. I cleaned up the baby, changed her diaper and outfit, and threw another romper in the diaper bag just in case. We hopped into our Volkswagen Rabbit and flew to church. Late.

I ate humble pie for Sunday supper that day.

Kids and the Clock

When it comes to being on top of our time, it certainly is more difficult with kids in the picture. Not only do we have to strategize just how and when we'll get *our* work done, we have to make sure that all the little (and not so little) people in our lives cooperate. Factor in a hubby, a family pet, the phone, the doorbell, and a telemarketer or two, and it's a wonder any of us ever gets any work done.

Now, at the risk of sounding like a broken record (uh…that shows my age! How about a skipping CD?), I want to make sure we have a worthy goal in mind for managing our time. Our motive should not be to wow everyone around us with how efficient we are. It should not be to get more done in a shorter amount of time so we can pile more "stuff" on our plates. Our motivation should be to free up time for the important things in life, the simple pleasures and unhurried moments with our loved ones that, looking back from the grave, we'll wish we could have experienced one more time. You've heard it said that no one ends her life wishing she'd spent more time at the office. How true! While putting in office time is a mandate for moms who must work outside the home and at-home moms often view their homes and vehicles as a sort of office, we certainly want to accomplish the tasks we can in the smartest and shortest way so we can get on to the fun!

Is your time stretched to the point of breaking? Are there not enough hours in your day or days in your week? How can this be?

To the world outside, moms at home seem to have it easy. I mean, what sounds more passive than "staying home" with your children. Think of the many ways that phrase is used to describe other situations:

"Did you go to the work day at the church grounds last week?"

"Nope. I stayed home."

"Are you going to brave the crowds and go Christmas shopping during the big day after Thanksgiving sale?"

"I don't think so. I'll just stay home."

Unfortunately, the phrase "stay home" can denote slacking off and doing nothing. Instead of saying a mom stays home, I prefer to phrase it that she *works* at home. Think about it. If she were at an outside job all day long, she couldn't leave her children unattended all day. Someone would have to get them up, dress them, feed them, cook, clean, change diapers, give naps, chauffer them, monitor homework, feed them again, clean up again, and so on and so on. What moms at home do all day is *work!* I know, especially when I had three small children at home with me all day long (including an infant and toddler), that the only time my fanny hit the sofa was to nurse the baby or read a naptime book.

To describe your busy, important life as a full-time mom as "just staying home" doesn't give an accurate description and sells yourself short. You are more than employed! I have yet to meet a mom, at home with young children, who takes an entire hour for lunch or clocks out at five o'clock. The term full-time mom even has lurking behind it notions of a forty-hour workweek, but that hardly scratches the surface. Nope, although 24/7 is an overused phrase, it is an accurate assessment of the time spent on the job by a mom at home.

Time Wasters

So what slows us moms down when it comes to managing our time in the home? We've already mentioned the darlin' dependents, and we'll talk about them more later. For now, let's deal with our own selves—personality traits, habits, actions, and inaction. What causes us to waste time and frolic away the hours when we should be making progress? Here are seven enemies of proper time management.

Procrastination

Yep, good ol' procrastination. We've all been defeated by it. Put off until tomorrow what should have been done today. Then tomorrow, instead of knuckling down and doing it, we delay just one more day. Yeah, tomorrow will be different. I'll make a fresh start of it. But alas, the next day the same scenario repeats. Pretty soon, the task is weeks (maybe months) overdue and we beat ourselves up for our failure to get it done.

If you are like most moms, you have either a physical or mental list of the projects you wish you had gotten around to actually doing: place photos in scrapbooks; reorganize the basement storage; clean out the kitchen cupboards; call my aunt who has cancer; sort through the kids' closets and dressers; tackle that pile of magazines; do a little landscaping out front; read that book; write that letter...and on and on it goes.

So we continue to push into the future many of our homemaking chores. We feel guilty. We let it hinder our sleep and spoil our fun. And we think if someone would just take our kids away for three full weeks, we could finally get caught up!

If you thought I was going to beat you up on this one, think again. While there are those of us who are persistent procrastinators, our problem with procrastination isn't always that we are slow to jump in and work. Sometimes it's because we have unrealistic expectations. Or we attempt to tackle too many projects at this season in life. Rather than determine that the activity just isn't for us to do right now and let it go, we mope and mumble to ourselves about how we just can't seem to get these items checked off our to-do list.

This happened to me four years ago, and I'm going to tell you about it in hope that it will help you. I am a little hesitant to share this story, and I want to say up front that I have nothing against scrapbooking consultants. Nor do I despise women who spend their Friday evenings gathered 'round the table with their circle of friends, deckle scissors in hand, smiles on their faces as they lovingly craft those beautiful scrapbooks that chronicle their children's childhoods.

I was even among their ranks, once upon a time. Many of my friends got into the scrapbooking scene when my children were young. Up until then I had been keeping all my photos in boxes filed in chronological order. When a box became full, I labeled it by year (or years) and began a new box. I thought I was doing a good thing. I already knew the perils of placing photos in those cheap, department store, peel-back laminate albums. I figured my system was working.

When Mackenzie was six, Mitchell three, and Spencer a newborn, the scrapbooking craze hit full force. My friend Michelle and I decided we were going to become official scrapbookers. We spent one entire summer, three days a week from just after breakfast until naptime was over in the late afternoon, working on putting our scrapbooks together. I should have clued in when I saw Michelle's gorgeous masterpieces next to my pitiful pages that this was not my gift. I am severely craft challenged. I have an aversion to art supplies, am allergic to glue guns, and can't sew to save my life.

But that summer I got "all caught up" and had each of the three kids' books current. It was then that it hit me:

> Oh no! What have I done? Now I'm going to have to keep this up until each of them graduates. That's over eighteen years! Do I really want to spend great chunks of my time doing this? I'm really not even good at it. I don't even enjoy scrapbooking. I simply like spending time with Michelle and feeling like I am accomplishing something that's helping me get organized. I never thought about having to keep this up for years on end. Maybe my old system was all right in the first place!

Thus began a period of about six years where I felt like an utter failure in this area. While other friends were happily clipping away, I was stressing that I hadn't found any time to work on scrapbooks at all. Because I am not someone who likes to leave projects lying out and slowly work on them a little at a time (this is one of my "ticks me off" items), I had to haul everything out and have a marathon scrapbooking session of at least eight to ten hours to "accomplish enough," which I rarely did. All the while, my procrastination made me feel like a failure. I even remember being in bed, dreading the thought of my daughter's graduation open house when I would be frantically trying to paste the last few pictures in her album for all to view while our guests munched on barbequed meatballs.

Finally I came to a bold conclusion. I was not cut out to do scrapbooks (pun intended). I don't enjoy it. I am lousy at it. I'd rather spend money on something else. I'd rather write a journal to each of my children. I also had to convince myself that it will not permanently damage my children if they don't have beautiful albums like their friends will someday. All my childhood photos are in an antique trunk at my mom's house, and I haven't needed professional therapy because of it.

Is there anything you are feeling a sense of dread over because it's remaining undone? Perhaps you should just cross it off your list and let it go!

With what's left on your list, ask yourself just why you are putting off doing each item. Could any task be done more easily with a friend or two? Time to call in the Amazon Women! Maybe it's one of those chores that if you just knuckle down and start, it wouldn't be so hard to finish after all. Many time-management experts assert that if you give yourself 15 minutes for a smaller task or an hour for a larger one and dive in, the sense of accomplishment you feel in the early stages of the project is enough to keep you going. I have found this to be totally true. Try it!

Mental Escapes

Good ol'-fashioned mental escape. This can be staring out a window and wishing you were somewhere else, wondering how much better it would be "if only…" It can come by way of the television and all the bold, beautiful people whose world is turning as they spend the days of their lives looking for love in the afternoon. Yes, many moms are addicted to soap operas. Rather than taking on the day-to-day living of their own lives, they prefer to cash out and tune in to someone else's fictitious life filled with excitement and glamor. I have friends who say breaking this addiction was harder than kicking a nasty health habit. If you want to quit, enlist the help of a friend who will hold you accountable. She can call you periodically to ask about your afternoon viewing habits. Plan to be out of the house when "your" particular show is on. Take the baby for a walk. Take the toddler to the park. Go to a friend's house who doesn't watch such shows. If you are wasting time by watching these shows or reading them in the form of romance novels, kick the habit!

Lack of Knowledge

What trips up many moms is lack of knowledge when it comes to managing time. No one has ever come alongside us and shown us how. If you are a former full-time working woman turned mom-at-home, you'll be especially thrown for a loop. In the "outside" working world days have structure—meeting at 9:30, lunch at 12:00, project due by 3:00, shift ends at 5:00. Stay-at-home moms are forced to create their own structure. When we just take the day as it comes, without being proactive in planning how we'd like it to stack up, we are left with piles of undone projects and confusion on the part of our kids and dear hubbies. There are no two ways about it: Moms at home need to know how to manage their minutes, hours, and days to full advantage.

Media Mania

Like daydreaming, even good media can rob us of our prime productive time each day. While I occasionally enjoy a radio talk show, a TV program, movie special, or, more frequently, a news magazine broadcast, I make sure I'm in control of the television, magazine reading, and recreational book reading instead of the other way around. Are there any programs or magazines you should give up to make more time for work and add order to your life?

Telephone and Computer

Some aspects of our modern-day culture are both blessings and curses when it comes to time. I often wonder what it would have been like to be an author 25 years ago before e-mail attachments and personal computers. Today I can shoot my manuscript across the nation to my publisher, and then, when changes are necessary, they shoot it back to me for corrections in seconds flat.

The telephone also enables us to transact business, catch up with our friends, and check on our kids quickly. It keeps us connected.

Both of these tools, however, can also serve as great hindrances to moms when it comes to time management. Left unchecked or without a plan and limits, we easily fritter away hours talking, whether with our mouths or our fingers, instead of tackling the tasks at hand. I've certainly done my fair share of frittering on the phone.

Beware, too, if you are a mom who is drawn to the Internet and the endless possibilities it offers surfers. Don't let this tool control your time. While you may think you're just going to hop on the computer for a quick search for a new recipe for lasagna, 1,320,000 items will be available for your viewing pleasure. Without you realizing it, the clock ticks away and now your family is ticked off, standing at the empty table waiting for something to eat.

Curb and curtail the communication tools in your life. Make them serve you instead of the other way around.

Laziness

There isn't a lot to say about this time waster. We all recognize when someone is being plain lazy. The teen who won't get up and get his yard work started; the elementary school child who would rather lie around and watch afternoon cartoons than do his homework; the moms who choose idleness rather than work. There's certainly nothing wrong with built-in breaks, such as taking a nap if your body really needs one or resting your brain for a while and doing something mindless. When we *habitually* do these things they become counter-productive.

Excessive Possessions

What? Owning too many things can waste time? You betcha! The more you own, the more that owns you. You spend time cleaning, maintaining, repairing, transporting, and using your stuff. Make sure you and your family prayerfully and carefully choose the items you will own. While there is nothing inherently wrong with installing a swimming pool on your property, owning a few snowmobiles for fun, or having the latest and greatest electronic gizmos, consider the time, energy, and money you'll expend to keep these things running and useful. Even seemingly innocent possessions consume our time, such as pets, gardens, extra bathrooms, and bigger yards. Choose your possessions wisely!

Paralyzed Perfectionism

Some women who tend to be detailed and thorough by nature have a syndrome I call "paralyzed perfectionism." These women want to tackle projects and do everything "right." If they can't do something perfectly, they won't start the project at all. Often they need to be reminded to...well...lighten up. Does it really matter if the oven is cleaned using your perfect seven-step process? Isn't it just imperative at this stage in your mothering that it's relatively clean? It doesn't have to be spotless to be used.

Plan Your Work and Work Your Plan

Once you have taken a look at your daily schedule, recognizing any commitments that need to go, what do you do? How do you make the most use of the time you have every day? Should you make out a list and follow it carefully?

Yes and no.

I don't know about you, but I have had a love/hate relationship with to-do lists. While I love to make them, I hate trying to get to the end of them, especially because I tend to overestimate how much I can get done in a certain amount of time. I also never factor in that someone may get sick, break an arm, tear her hair out working on a science project, get an earring embedded in a body part (don't ask) and need a trip to the emergency room. When I have 18 tasks on my list, and at the end of the day I have only crossed off 3, I feel like a failure.

Lately I split my list into what I have to do and what I would like to do. I list those things that must be done by nightfall, and if I get to the other chores, fine. I keep this list on a clipboard to refer to easily during the day. To take a look at the daily to-do sheet I use, see page 225. It also has a space labeled "To Buy." This is not an exhaustive grocery list. We'll tackle that in chapter 8. This is a small space the size of a Post-it. Place a Post-it over that space, and if you think of any items you need between shopping trips—*Oops, ran out of toilet paper. Better stop at the store*—you can jot them down here. Pull off that Post-it for reference when you head out.

My daily task sheet also lists who I need to call, e-mail, or write a note to. There is also a small section labeled "Don't Forget." Here I list thoughts that pop into my mind: "Don't forget to ask mom what day we are celebrating Uncle Kevin's birthday." "Ask Tammy for that new low-fat cranberry muffin recipe." I also note upcoming events: "Don't forget the fall Art Fest is the second Saturday in October." When updating my calendar, I check this space to see if I need to record times or dates.

Caution: Don't let your list be your taskmaster. Don't allow it to dictate your mood depending on what you do and don't cross off. Although the list can serve as your GPS, there are times when God will divert you from your projected tasks and ask you to accomplish something more important for him. The key is recognizing when the interruptions in your day are sent by God.

There have been days when I haven't gotten to the items on my list because God sent a sick child, a wounded friend, or a lonely neighbor to my side. At the end of such a day, I've taken a red pen and in large letters written, "Hold a sick, feverish child, comforting him and supplying him with Popsicles. All other tasks temporarily on divine hold."

I picture these "interruptions" as the hand of God. He is diverting me from my lowly plan to his perfect plan for my day. I trust there will be time to finish what I wanted to do (or thought I needed to do) later. More often than not, I am pleased with the way things turn out.

I've learned over the years that it does no good to stew all day about the loss of my time. As my husband says, "It didn't surprise God!" God knew what interruption would come, what delay I'd experience; truth be told, he allowed it for my good. So should you make a list and follow it carefully? Yes and no. Use it as a guide, but know when to set it aside.

Crafting a Plan

"Should you plan your work and then work your plan?" Much like the schedule question, the answer is yes and no. A plan is different from a daily task list. A plan is a strategy for accomplishing your work in the home. While a list might include short tasks such as bathe the dog, take out the trash, bake a cake, mop the entryway, a work plan puts a logical order to the tasks at hand, assuring they can be accomplished in the most efficient manner.

While I am all for having a proactive plan for the various aspects of the mission of motherhood, let's remember that we'll often be sidetracked to another matter or a child needing attention. So I advocate having a plan, but I urge you to not panic and fret when it doesn't come off without a hitch.

Your Proactive Plan

We're making progress! Now for a proactive plan. As much as I'd like to take credit for this idea, I'm not its originator. I first learned about it many years ago from a well-known author. When Mackenzie was young, she simply adored Laura Ingalls Wilder. I read a portion of the Little House on the Prairie series to her each afternoon before her nap. Once she could read, I bought her the illustrated, early reader versions. Years later, one afternoon when she was helping me by getting both of her younger brothers down for a nap, I wandered by her room and heard her reading:

In the morning, Ma would begin the particular task that belonged to that day. Ma would say: wash on Monday, iron on Tuesday, mend on Wednesday, churn on Thursday, clean on Friday, bake on Saturday, rest on Sunday.

Eureka! That's it! I needed to do what Ma Ingalls did and divide my chores over the days of the week. Wilder's character probably never attended a seminar on home organization. She followed a routine passed down by previous generations of women. I needed to take a cue from them, and I'm suggesting you do too.

There is no "right" way to make a plan. It can be as detailed or as basic as you want. If you want to be really thorough, spell out a daily, monthly, and yearly proactive plan. If that much detail sets your head spinning, opt for a scaled-down version. You can write your plan on a large index card, in a notebook, or type it on your computer complete with color and clip art.

What works best for me is to write my plan on 8½ x 11-inch paper so it can be part of what I call my "brain in a binder." (I will be explaining this in the next chapter.) I put the paper in a clear page protector. That way, it doesn't get splattered or stained, and I can use a wax pencil or marker to check off the tasks once they are completed. Then, the next time I use it, I simply wipe it off and start over.

A Daily Plan

When I first began doing this years ago, I needed a "Ma Ingalls" plan in the worst way. Remember, I was the mom who couldn't seem to get a shower done by noon. I had no structure in my days, no logical plan of what I should be trying to accomplish each day. I needed a daily target to shoot for. So I got out an index card and spelled it out. After rearranging and readjusting, what I came up with looked something like this for my first plan:

- Read Bible and pray.
- Make bed and pick up bedroom.

- Eat breakfast and take vitamins.
- Shower and dress.
- Wipe down bathroom sink and counter (in case anyone stopped over and needed to use bathroom while visiting).
- Thaw any meat needed for supper or assemble main dish or make dessert, if needed. (You want to think of that in the morning hours, not at 4:30 P.M.!)
- Daily task for the day:
  - Monday: laundry
  - Tuesday: grocery shop
  - Wednesday: laundry
  - Thursday: bills and paperwork
  - Friday: laundry
  - Saturday: clean house
- Eat lunch.
- Afternoon: naptime, run errands.
- Evening: eat supper, load, run, and empty the dishwasher.
- Pick up stray items in house before bed.
- Pack Todd leftovers for tomorrow's lunch.

My plan helped to jog my memory and prevent some of those household scenarios that "tick me off" we discussed in chapter 2. It ticks me off to wake up to dirty dishes in the sink. Making "load, run, and empty the dishwasher" one of the last tasks of my day helped prevent that situation most days. After years of use, I no longer need such an exhaustive list. I have a scaled back version listing only the items I tend to forget to do, like take my vitamins.

Getting the Kids Involved

You may also want your kids to each have a plan. We try to operate by the "work before play" principle at our house. It gives all involved, both parents and kids, incentive to finish their chores so we can do something fun. If your children aren't able to read yet, make a visual plan for them to follow.

Using your computer's clip art program, create a page with the pictures of the various tasks they need to complete each morning before breakfast or each evening before going to bed. You can use pictures of someone making a bed, brushing teeth, getting dressed, combing hair. Your kids simply need to glance at the page to see what they need to do next. We did this for our youngest child, Spencer. We taped the paper to the underneath side of the top bunk where he was sure to see it since he slept in the bottom bunk. It was a daily, visual reminder to him to get up and get at it.

If you want to step it up a notch and you're a shutterbug mom, take pictures! Gather the kids and have them enact the very chores they are required to do each day while you snap pictures of them. Glue them to brightly colored poster board, and cover with clear contact paper. Place this in a location where they can refer to it while they carry out their routines. Using a visual plan for kids sure beats nagging. Instead of telling your children over and over "Go brush your teeth!" simply say, "Go check the picture plan. Have you finished your routine yet?"

Periodically, when your kids are doing well following their routines for several days or weeks, reward them. Let them invite a friend over to play. Take them to the store to pick out a small item. Drive through McDonald's for an unexpected ice-cream cone. When the kids ask why the surprise, tell them, "I've noticed how you've really been doing your daily routine without being asked. This is my way of thanking you. It really makes mom's job a lot easier, and don't you love that I don't need to yell and holler anymore?" (At least that last phrase is spoken at my house!)

A Monthly Plan

Next we have a monthly proactive plan. Place this on your next index card or piece of paper in your binder. This will divvy up chores that only need to be performed once or twice a month. Here is an example:

Monthly Chores

Week 1: Clean oven.

Week 2: Wash and clean out van.

Week 3: Change and wash sheets.

Week 4: Wash windows.

You may choose different chores for your list: clean the floors, straighten up the garage, weed the flower beds, defragment the computer, and so on. Having these tasks listed reminds you to tackle them before they reach unmanageable stages. On Sunday evenings, I sit down and look over the coming week's schedule. I look for pockets of time when I can pencil in these monthly tasks. Let's say I'll be in town because of the kids' guitar lessons, and Spencer and I will need to kill an hour. If my chore for that week is to wash and clean out the van, we can pop over to the coin-operated car wash. While I clean out and vacuum the van, Spencer can spray the water, pretending it's a Star Wars light saber! My task is easily slipped into my routine.

A Yearly Plan

Finally, let's chart a yearly proactive plan. This is where we plan bigger chores that need attention once a year or so. You can also list anything here that will help you stay ahead of the game. For example, I need to get my yearly physical each July. Let's say it takes three months to get an appointment. So one of my April tasks can be "make yearly exam appointment."

Here is my sample yearly proactive plan:

January: Write Christmas thank-you notes; dejunk the house.

February: Purge all files; get tax documents together.

March: Wash miniblinds and curtains.

April: Rearrange furniture, clean carpets; make Mom's yearly exam appointment.

May: Clean out garage; get out summer clothes.

June: Plant herbs and flowers.

July: Plan and order curriculum.

August: Dejunk the house; reorganize schoolroom.

September: Trim shrubs; make Dad's yearly doctor appointment.

October: Clean out garage; get out winter clothes.

November: Rearrange furniture for Christmas tree; clean carpets.

December: Holiday tasks; touch up paint on the walls.

All these plan charts are the start of our "brain in a binder." I'll explain more in the next chapter what else goes into this useful tool. If coming up with such a flexible routine on paper would benefit you, take a few minutes in the next day or so to craft your own proactive plan. Remember, these aren't meant to be strict rigid schedules. *They are flexible routines that allow for interruptions from God and ministry to others.* They will help you keep your days, weeks, months, and year on track.

To Multitask or Not?

The final question in the handling of our time is one many moms have posed to me. To multitask or not to multitask? Again the answer is yes and no.

We are experts at multitasking. We can be talking on the phone, cooking supper, French-braiding hair, correcting homework, and nursing a baby all at the same time. The ability to multitask can be a blessing. However, there are times when it can be a curse. The key is knowing when to use this wonderful tool in a mom's organizational toolbox and when to focus on one thing.

For example, when you have spots in your day where you'll be spending time waiting, it's beneficial to think of one or more additional tasks you could be performing. If you are in the orthodontist's office waiting for a child to have her monthly checkup, it would be smart to bring along something to do: write a few birthday or anniversary cards; fill out that permission slip for a field trip or medical form for a sports team. It helps to have these items inside a plastic clipboard with a compartment for storing such papers. (We'll talk more about making a clipboard part of your daily routine in chapter 7.)

Where else do you have waiting time to multitask? Can you return library books and do your banking while you're waiting for a child at a music lesson? If you're a homeschool mom, can you correct papers during this time? Besides such waiting times, are there other windows of opportunity to combine tasks and free up more time? Can you fold laundry while taking care of business on the phone, especially when it's a call where you may be on hold for a while? Can you clean the bathroom while supervising the toddler in the tub? If you brainstorm, I'm sure you can come up with dozens of ways to do two or three tasks at once. Let's just see if any of you can beat one of my friend Suzy's best ones. One day when I called to ask her a question, I discovered she was bleaching her teeth, exercising by jumping on her mini trampoline, and administering a spelling test all at the same time!

Yes, there is a wrong time to multitask too. It's when other people are involved who need your undivided attention. They can tell when we're not really focusing on them because we're performing another task. This is where many feelings get hurt and inadvertent mistakes are made.

My child may feel slighted because I'm not *really* listening to her tale. Perhaps she's telling me about the picture she colored or the funny thing that happened to her and her friend at the store. I nod and smile, but she knows I'm not really listening. I have something else that is demanding my attention—like the meal I'm making or the laundry

I'm folding. Tell me—can't those chores wait while I stop, look my child in the eye, and listen to her for five or ten minutes? The chores will still be there when I'm done.

Wounded feelings aside, the other peril of not listening is the possibility of inadvertently saying yes to a child's question when we should have said no. This usually happens to me because I'm trying to listen while I'm talking on the phone. All of a sudden, my son heads off to do something I gave him permission to do by mistake.

We must think carefully about our multitasking efforts. Use this tool only when it won't get in the way of your relationship with your child and when it won't backfire!

Finally, what has been the most helpful for me in getting my time under control has been learning to reorder my week. Rather than making Sunday a leftover, catch-up day when I fold laundry and tackle piles of paper, I make it my focal point of the week. I work toward getting all my work done *before* Sunday. Making Sunday a time off from our regular routine is wonderfully refreshing! God's ideas are best, and it was his idea to make Sundays a day of rest. Doesn't it energize you to think about having fifty-two days off from your regular work routine at home? We can worship, rest, play, and nap! I know of no better way to order your week. Try it. You won't want to go back to your old routine.

As you continue your quest for calm and order, be intentional and strategic in how you use your time. Take care of the "have to's" of life in an efficient manner so your time is free for the "want to's." Then you'll be able to spend unhurried time with loved ones. Although you won't always have your to-do list items all checked off at the end of each day, you'll have time to take care of all God planned for you each day.

What Works for Me

Melinda Walker, South Carolina

I admit it—I have a routine for every possible aspect of my life. And if I have to depart from my routines, I'm a little lost. I have routines for mornings, writing, laundry, meals, evenings, shopping, weekends, and cleaning. Routines just don't happen, though; they require planning. Each one has to be formulated and implemented. There are shopping and to-do lists to create. Most difficult of all, your family members have to be trained. But the benefits make it worthwhile. Here's how routines help:

- They save wear and tear on my scattered brain.

- I get to be involved in some evening activities because my husband and children know what to do next while I'm gone.

- *I* know what to do next.

- Out-of-control situations (needed clothes not clean, needed items not purchased, dirt/mess buildup, etc.) occur occasionally rather than frequently.

Make routines work for you!

What Works for Me

Marianne Stuart, Michigan

I handle the morning school rush by enlisting my husband's help. He came up with the idea, and the kids for some reason love it. He calls it "Line Up." The kids have to be ready at 8:00 A.M. each school morning. They line up in age order, and Dad asks each child the following questions:

- Have you eaten breakfast?

- Have you brushed your teeth?

- Have your brushed your hair?

- Do you have clean clothes on?

- Is your bed made?

- Is your morning chore done?

If anyone is late for Line Up or hasn't done part of his or her morning duties, that child is given push-ups or sit-ups. The "Drill Sergeant" always gives push-ups for smiling. I don't know why. The kids and my husband love this morning routine. I get to come down and see the kitchen clean and the kids ready and smiling. If my husband has to leave early, I do Line Up, but I dole out push-ups for not smiling!

What Works for Me

Cindy Sigler Dagnan, Missouri, from her wonderful book
Who Got Peanut Butter on My Daily Planner?

The oasis principle. Make your bed as soon as you wake up every morning. Teach your children to do the same. No matter how crazy or cluttered your day is, there will always be a spot of calm. Try to make one oasis spot in every room: the kitchen table, the coffee table, the bathroom counter, the top of the filing cabinet. Make it a habit to live by the motto "Everything has a home."

7

PUTTING PAPER IN ITS PLACE

• •

Ah yes…paper. Is there any aspect of maintaining an uncluttered home that is more unnerving? Sure, the kitchen may get messy. So what! We can always clean it up again, wiping and scrubbing until the counter is clean, the dishes are done, and the pots and pans are back in their places.

But paper is a whole different ball game. While we may be able to spend an afternoon sorting, purging, and pitching unnecessary piles of paper, it's only a temporary fix. No sooner have we tossed our piles into the trash (or recycle bin) than a whole new batch enters our homes. Paper comes at us from all directions. The newspaper arrives. The mail gets delivered. The kids return home from school or an extracurricular activity with papers. Because we aren't always sure what to do with all this communication, we end up placing it neatly in piles.

Did I say "neatly"? Now, come on! Do *neat* piles actually exist? I'm not sure I've ever seen one. Okay, maybe I've seen a few, but they didn't stay neat for long. As soon as someone needs a paper thought to be hiding in said pile, she rifles through it and leaves it a complete mess.

And what do these perpetual piles of paper do to us moms? They shout, "Failure, failure, failure! Look at you, Mom. You don't know where to put us, so you choose any horizontal surface and plop us down. Incompetent! Can't you even take care of the paper in your home, for crying out loud?"

Okay, so maybe I've never actually had a pile of paper talk to me like an apple tree on the way to Oz, but I have had that exact line of thought run through my brain. Piles are defeating. They remind me that I'm not on top of my game. I didn't have a plan for those papers, so there they sit. They are the culmination of the "for now's" in my life. You know, I'll set this mail here *for now*. I'll put these papers on the counter *for now*. I really don't have time to think about what to do with these clothes, shoes, toys, store items, so I'll just lay them here *for now*. *For now* derails our organization train!

Not all women who are "pilers" are unorganized. Some view their piles as horizontal files. They know exactly where papers are located. Perhaps their dining room tables are strewn with stacks of paper. Someone asks if she has seen the current issue of a favorite magazine that should have arrived in the mail by now. "Of course!" she'll answer. She'll stroll over to her file cabinet (her dining room table) and locate the periodical. "Let's see now...third pile from the right about halfway down...Voilá! Here it is!"

Yep, some pilers are very organized. It's their method, and it works for them. Apparently piles don't bother them. However, others find it hard to function in this manner. If you're an organized piler, I suggest you flip your horizontal piles and turn them into vertical files. That way when family members need to unearth a paper, they will have greater luck at locating it.

For a while I attacked my piles this way: I would set aside an hour or so a week to deal with my pile of paper. (I did try to keep it down to one pile on my old "card table turned work station.") I'd wade through the pile and make several smaller piles: bills, fliers, letters needing to be answered, items I needed to file away for future use, and, of course, paper headed for the recycle bin. Then I would put all those subpiles away. This helped out in the short run. However, if I missed a week or two, the mountain of paper was so overwhelming I would almost cry just thinking about tackling it.

Each time I sorted it, I noticed that, without fail, the tallest pile when I was all done was the "pitch it" pile. It never occurred to me that if I pitched those papers the day they arrived, I'd only need to touch them once instead of twice. This would streamline the process and keep my pile smaller.

After this revelation I began sorting my mail over the recycle can each afternoon when it arrived (and now we finally own a paper shredder to do this over). Into the shredder went credit-card applications, junk mail, and circulars from stores I don't shop at. It was a giant step and really helped trim the size of the weekly pile.

Soon I discovered more tricks and tools that comprise the Pile Busting 101 class you are about to take. I'm sure that just the notion of making those annoying piles disappear sends shivers of glee coursing through your entire body. Before you jump for joy, let me give it to you straight: No area is easier to organize but harder to keep on top of than piles of paper.

You heard me right. It's simple to set up a system, but hard to master. There are many ways to deal with paper. Some are overcomplicated, and others are relatively simple. Once you spend the time to get a plan in place, the problem doesn't magically disappear. The trick is to stay on top of it. Due to the fact that you'll continue to have papers flying your way at least six days a week (through the mail if through nothing else), you'll have to be steady in following-through on your plan.

Pile Busting 101

So let's start! First of all, here are a few basic components you'll need in order to complete the setup process:

- A highlighter or pen with bright ink. Find a fun one! Inform the family that this is mom's special pen, and no one is to mess with it. Violators will be prosecuted!

- A 1- to 1½-inch binder. (I like the ones with a clear sleeve on the front where you can insert a photo or scrapbooking page.)

- Your mission statement and any pages you crafted for your proactive plans

- Enough 8½ x 11-inch, clear page protectors to hold your mission statement and proactive plans

- Some sturdy, three-hole-punched folders—enough for one per family member (I like the plastic or vinyl versions.)

- Some plain white computer labels

These components will be the start to what I fondly refer to as my "brain in a binder." It's one of three components to our paper-control system. The second is a file cabinet or box. For that you'll need:

- A filing cabinet or box, whether stationary or portable. This can be a traditional file cabinet or portable plastic file boxes designed to hold hanging folders.

- Hanging file folders. If you're a color-coding person, then by all means get the latest and prettiest shades if you like. You'll be using them for different categories of papers.

Finally, you need a plastic or metal clipboard that has a compartment for storing papers. They come in a variety of colors and styles. Select one that suits your fancy.

With these tools you're ready to begin. You'll spend an hour or so setting this up, but oh the peace that will follow! So let's get this system in place so we can work the system and save you work!

Pile Busting 101 gives you three places to put your downsized piles.

(You've already shredded or tossed the junk mail, papers you no longer need, etc.) First, the papers and periodicals that need to be stored for the long term go into your filing cabinet or portable file boxes in hanging folders. Call this your *permanent files*. Place your hanging file folders in your filing cabinet or box. Decide what files you'll need for long-term storage. A sampling of mine:

- Family tree information
- Manuals
- Taxes
- Past publications
- Warrantees
- Writing ideas

Whenever you come across an item that belongs in this long-term storage location, pull out the correct folder (or make a new one if it's something you haven't had to file before) and place the item in the folder. Periodically weed out these folders—once every year or so is sufficient since you're most likely only placing items in these folders that you want to keep for a long time. If an appliance or gadget breaks and is no longer usable, pitch the corresponding manual. Tax records need to be kept for seven years. Some people keep them ten to be safe.

The second category is *short-term files*. These are papers you may need to refer to over the next few weeks and months but then will most likely toss. We'll place these in our "brain in a binder."

This "brain in a binder" has enabled me to greatly reduce the clutter at our house. It's a binder designed to keep your short-term files at your fingertips. I have known many women who use various folder systems to keep their papers in one place. After much trial and error, I came up with this one.

In the front of the 1- to 1½-inch binder, place several clear page protectors. Into these clear protectors put any of the following in any order you wish.

- Mother's mission statement you wrote
- Daily proactive plan
- Monthly proactive plan
- Yearly proactive plan
- Kids' daily routines

Behind these, place as many sturdy, three-hole-punched folders as you need to organize your family's papers. Label them with computer labels or peel-and-stick name tags. I have one that says "Family," three more—each with a different child's name on it—and one that says "Speaking." Into these I slip flyers, invitations, e-mails, maps, class lists, team rosters, sports schedules, directions to women's groups I am speaking at, and any papers I may need to refer to in the near future. They all go into the folders, divided according to the family member they relate to.

Modify this system in a way that makes sense for your family. Maybe you'll want a single folder for Mom and Dad. Perhaps you'll want to have just two folders, one labeled "This Month" and one marked "Future." My friend Leah has thirty-one clear page protectors, one for each day of the month, and pops her family's papers into the day it pertains to. I am not that detailed; perhaps you are.

The folders keep my calendar looking neater because, instead of trying to squeeze into a small box on my calendar or planner all the info about a particular event, I write the event and time on the proper square on my calendar or planner and put the actual invitation in the folder labeled "Mom." When it's time to shop for a gift or drive to the shower, all I need to do is grab my "brain in a binder" and retrieve the invitation to read anything I need to know.

To help the entire family keep track of events and dates, I write brief information from the various schedules—sports, school, church—and planned family events on a family wall calendar. Some moms color-code these entries: blue for the family, red for one child, green for another, and so on. I prefer to write in my calendar/planner and on my wall calendar in pencil. That way if plans change, the schedule doesn't end up looking nasty with cross-outs.

This tool reduces parental headaches. If it's my turn to make treats for my boy's homeschool co-op class on a Friday, I simply turn to the proper folder to see how many students are in the class. If my son's ride suddenly falls through for Little League practice, I can easily flip to his folder, pull out the team roster, and call another parent to see if my son can carpool with her that night.

My kids also love this folder system. If they need to know any information about one of their clubs, sports, or organizations, they can grab the binder and look at the needed paper. But they know the two most important rules: (1) put the paper back in the proper folder once you've looked at it, and (2) no one removes the binder from mom's desk! These directives are to be strictly adhered to.

This "brain in a binder" doesn't need much upkeep. It usually is pretty good at weeding itself out. When an event is over, toss the invitation. Is it the end of a season? Pitch the papers for the sports that are through. But take note if it's something you may need to refer to in the future. I keep my once-used MapQuest directions for places I may need to go again in our van's glove compartment.

I really encourage you to try this "brain in a binder" at least for a few months. It's actually kind of fun to put together. You can even have an Amazon Women night where you and a few friends go out for coffee to brainstorm, make a trip to the office supply store, and then swing by the grocers to get a few pints of your favorite ice cream or some salty snacks. Add your favorite soft drinks, and you're ready to work. Don't forget to bring along some pictures of your clan and a few scrapbooking supplies to make a clever cover for the front (and back, if you wish!).

Perhaps you'll want to add even more to your binder. That's great! Customize it in a way that works for you. Some gals like to purchase 8½ x 11-inch calendar pages from an office supply store and put these into their binders. You can add an address book or a three-hole-punched notepad. Make this tool personalized to keep you on top of things and help alleviate those dreadful piles.

Finally, we have those items that need to be dealt with today. These papers make up your *hot file,* and some are truly smokin'. If we inadvertently misplace these items, we often uncover them too late, sometimes causing us embarrassment and even money in the form of late fees and fines. Keep the hot file safe and visible in your handy compartment clipboard.

I'll bet there isn't a woman within the sound of my pounding keyboard who hasn't dealt with a lost permission slip or a late library book or DVD rental. This clipboard keeps these events to a minimum. On the outside of the clipboard do what suits your fancy. If you want to clip a pad to it with a running list of your hot tasks, fine. If you'd like a little more detailed list, check out the reproducible daily task sheet on page 225 that was explained in chapter 6. This can help you by serving as a guide (not a master!) as you go about your day.

Working the System

So let's walk through this system. When you sort through your mail or any of the other papers that enter your home through a child or hubby, do it over a recycle bin or paper shredder. Any junk items go straight into the recycle bin or shredder. Don't even open that credit-card application. Shred it! No, you don't need another amazing piece of exercise equipment or a rubber stamp with your return address on it. Pitch these pieces immediately!

For the remaining articles ask yourself these questions:

- *Do I need to deal with this today?* If so, open it, circle or highlight any necessary information, and place it in your clipboard compartment. You'll want to take care of it by nightfall. If your child brings home a permission slip for a field trip, tuck it into the clipboard compartment. Did you receive a notice in the mail of a bill that is due, and you don't want to forget and be charged a late fee? Slip that in too. A notice from the library that junior's book was due two days ago? Put that in with the other today papers. Use your handy colored pen or highlighter to emphasize pertinent information on these papers—dates, addresses, etc. Make checking your clipboard compartment each night before retiring a habit. Deal with anything that must be dealt with right then.

- *Should this be filed in long-term storage?* If yes, file it right then. If you absolutely can't stop and file it right then, place it in your clipboard. You'll take care of it before nightfall.

- *Is this a flyer or information sheet for a family member's activity?* Put it in the proper folder in your "brain in a binder." Be sure to copy any times or dates to your personal calendar and family wall calendar first.

- *Is this for my husband or child?* Put it in an agreed-upon location for them to deal with it.

- *Is this a magazine or personal letter I want to read at my leisure?* You can choose a few locations for these items. Perhaps you have a basket in your living room for reading material. When you get a break in your day, saunter over to the basket, pull out the magazine or letter, and enjoy reading it. I love to read personal mail and the few magazines I get, so I motivate myself to finish my housework by not opening any of these items when they arrive. Then, when I'm doing well with my daily routine, I stop to have a cup of tea or coffee and read these items then. You can also store these items in a folder or tote bag and grab it when you're on your way to a place where you know you may be waiting for a while—the carpool line, soccer practice, or orthodontist's office.

- *Is this none of the above?* Decide just what it is and

where it should go. The key is not to simply toss it in one of those infamous "for now" piles in your house. You have a place for everything. Now put everything in its place.

Playing Paper Defense

Now that the system is in place for dealing with your papers, how do we manage to stay on top of it? What actions can we take daily to keep our papers in files instead of in piles on our counters, dressers, tables, and floors? Let's start by dealing with the main culprit—the trusty U.S. mail.

Six days a week a postal worker "blesses" us with an assortment of precious and pestering papers. It's estimated that every year each member of your family receives 230 pieces of unsolicited mail. In our family that totals over 1,000 pieces per year! When allowed to pile up, it takes up a lot of space and creates headaches. When my mom recently returned from two weeks in Florida, she faced a pile of mail more than a foot tall! Many of us have piles even more towering. How can we stop this?

For starters, send a postcard or make a phone call to the Direct Marketing Association (DMA). DMA claims to be the oldest and largest trade association of over 3,000 direct-mail firms, catalogers, publishers, retailers, and service organizations. Go to their Internet site: www.the-dma.org. Click on "Remove my name from mailing lists" in the upper-right corner. (There may be a nominal fee.) This will stop most, but not all, of those annoying credit-card applications, junk mailings, and catalogs for trinkets and treasures you don't want or need. DMA removal will not block mail from companies with whom you occasionally do business.

As for the other papers that fly your way from church, community, and school, be ruthless. When in doubt, throw it out. If you aren't sure you'll need the paper, want to buy the product with the clever coupon, or read the store flyer, let it fly. Also, give yourself some time to adjust to this new method for managing your paper. It will seem strange to not just toss the daily mail on the dining room table. In fact, at first it might seem like a hassle to sort and purge every day. But hold tight, dear one! No longer will you have to deal with setting aside an entire afternoon devoted to tackling piles of paper in your home. You can go do something fun instead!

Realistically, this system won't work without an occasional backup and some bumps in the road. It's a compass, a guide, a personal GPS. It points us in the right direction. It keeps us coming back to the intended path of less clutter. It is *not* our master, and we are not its slaves. It is here to serve us. Yes, you'll still have occasional, temporary, *small* piles of paper. For this I suggest a roll-top desk.

My husband bought me my first one, a secondhand beauty, 15 years ago. Best investment we ever made.

What Works for Me

Diana Brunett, Michigan

I buy boxed kids' birthday cards from Current or Family Christian Stores. I have an accordion-style file folder with dividers for each month. Written on the monthly dividers are the dates of my nieces' and nephews' birthdays. Every year, I find a card I like for each one's birthday from the boxes I purchased. I place it in the appropriate month, lightly writing in pencil on the envelope the person's name to whom the card will go.

Buying in quantity saves money, and I always have extras on hand for birthday parties that my daughters are invited to. Having it organized in advance ensures that I don't send the same card to a child and to a sibling. To make sure I remember to send the cards, I write each birthday in my daily planner, and a few days before the birthday, I write "mail card" in my planner.

I also have other greeting cards stockpiled and organized

upright in a shoebox (without the lid), so when I need a get-well card or other greeting card on short notice, I have many to choose from that I can get into the mail that day.

What Works for Me

Laura O'Conner, Michigan

I use colored folders to organize my family's papers. I keep them on my kitchen counter, readily available. We have tons of school papers, soccer schedules, coupons, doctor papers, things to do, checks to cash, receipts to log, birthday party invitations—you name it. Each member of my family has a different colored folder. The person's name is on the front. On the inside, I mark the left pocket "frequently viewed" and the right pocket "to do." Even my two-year-old has a folder. Lately, his contained doctor's records that I needed to view throughout the week. My five-year-old has his soccer schedule in the left pocket to reference each week and papers or notes in the right pocket that need to be addressed or replied to.

A simple system, but it works for me!

What Works for Me

Mitchell Ehman

You might like an idea that my mom thought of and gave to me for Christmas one year. It was a bookmark. But it wasn't just any bookmark. It was one she made and laminated herself that listed the phone numbers of my favorite stores. These were the ones I usually bugged her to look up for me when I wanted to call and see who had the best price on archery equipment or basketball shoes. This bookmark also has listed on it Web sites I sometimes visit. It saves time and keeps me from bothering Mom.

Mom's Management Central

While motherhood certainly is a mission, it benefits us to also look at some parts of it as a job or career. Maybe part of the reason you have been frustrated in your job as a mom has been that you have no office. I know for many of you your office has four wheels and is rolling down the highway most of the time. How about setting up a space in your home where you can tackle some of the logistics of motherhood and have everything you need within reach?

While not everyone can afford the luxury of a separate room, a corner or even a portable work station can serve as an office. My first work station was an old card table in our basement, along with a cork board purchased from a yard sale and a portable file box. I kept these items in a corner of the room and retreated there when I needed to get some work done. Although it was neither state of the art nor lovely to look at, that first "office" helped me get organized. When setting up your own work station, include any of the following you need in your role as mom and manager.

- A chair and a desk, table, or work surface.

- If you don't have a desk with drawers, you'll need cubbies and baskets for the top of the table and a portable file box or two. Pick ones that are designed to hold hanging folders.

- The basic office supplies: tape, stapler, paper, note-pads, pens, highlighters, pencils, and so forth.

- An address book.

- A calendar: wall, desk-style, or personal planner. Hearts at Home sells a "Just for Moms" planner. It's a desk-size, personal planner designed for moms. It contains sections including week-at-a-glance, month-at-a-glance, menu-and-grocery planner, home-and-family section, as well as a contact section for your family's needed phone numbers and addresses. Check it out at www.hearts-at-home.org.

- Some sort of bill-paying system. You can purchase a ready-made one from an office supply store or Internet site, or make your own. I use a binder with several three-ring-punched folders inside. I label them: Bills Due Now, Bills Due Soon, Stamps and Return Address Labels, Insurance Info, Tax Receipts, Miscellaneous. When a bill arrives, I put it in the proper folder in the binder. Then I get out the binder every Thursday to pay what is currently due. In this day and age, you can opt to pay your bills online. Familiarize yourself with companies you deal with that offer this service, and make it work to your advantage. It can save you time, stamps, and overdue penalties!

- Your "brain in a binder," if you make one. (I tend to keep this near the kitchen since I refer to it so often. On weekends it goes back in my "office.")

- A picture of your family and, perhaps, a copy of your mission statement.

8

MENU PLANNING AND SHOPPING STRATEGIES

• •

Next to handling paper, I have found that following a workable system for menu planning, grocery shopping, cooking, and clean-up is probably a mom's biggest challenge. Moms today know much less about meal planning and preparation than their mothers' and grandmothers' generations. This seems odd, considering that we have so many more foods to work with. I doubt that the supermarkets of former decades had the assortment of spices, the variety of apples, or the many brands of sugar we have today, but moms and grandmas could certainly bake better apple pies!

And think of all the other tools we have in this generation. We can turn on the television and have a world-renowned chef teach us his or her tricks of the trade. We have holiday hotlines available to answer questions about stuffing, basting, and carving Thanksgiving birds. We can hop on the Internet and search for oodles of recipes in three seconds flat. So why can't we get our act together in the kitchen?

Is it because we can't bake and cook...and lack the motivation to learn how? Are we too busy to plan and execute a nice evening meal? Do we loathe doing dishes? Are we embarrassed to be known as a kitchen whiz, assuming that only boring housewives busy themselves with such matters and real women are above being a Becky Homecky?

Whatever your reason for needing a little assistance in this room of the house, I hope you find some solutions to food-prep problems as we move on to this area.

When I first got married, I knew very little about cooking. I knew how to boil water, make instant coffee, and occasionally turn out a batch of my specialty: tasty slice-and-bake cookies from my local grocery store. I had to learn how to cook—and fast. You see, I married a man whose mother and three sisters all knew their way around the kitchen. One of them even went on to own a successful bed-and-breakfast. The bake-and-take Sara Lee pie I was hoping to take to the family function wasn't going to cut it no matter how much Cool Whip I dolloped on it.

I began my quest for cooking knowledge to keep up with the Joneses...er...um...the Ehmans. Funny thing is, *they* never saw it as a competition; only *I* did. They served as wonderful mentors in this area for me. Before taking the last name of Ehman, I'd never eaten a black olive or a piece of fish other than the stick form and an occasional tuna sandwich. I'd never used any herbs besides salt and pepper (are those even herbs?) or made real whipped cream in a chilled metal bowl with beaters. It was Cool Whip all the way for me. Even though my cooking journey began on the wrong foot, I've made great strides and gathered lots of tips to be more than proficient in the kitchen. I'm going to pass them on to you.

Finding Your Groove

Much like in the "Finding Your Organizational Personality" chapter, you need to think through what your goals are in this area. They won't be the same as your neighbor's, or your sister-in-law's, or even your best friend's. Women perform at various points along the cooking spectrum, from servers of frozen meals to gourmet cooks. Most gals are looking for a basic game plan, one that will enable them to plan their menus, shop easily, and cook great-tasting food for their families, all within monetary and time budgets. They know this means they'll have to check the grocery store ads, find out which meats, veggies, and fruits are on sale, and plan their menus accordingly.

Some women simplify the basic plan even more. They have weekly menus that they use over and over again. Monday's dinner is lasagna. Tuesday's is meatloaf. On Wednesday spaghetti is always served. Thursday's fare is chicken and noodles, and Friday night nachos rounds out the weekdays. On Saturday they dine on leftovers or go out for a bite to eat. Sunday dinner is always a roast and potatoes. This simple plan works for them. Their families aren't fussy and don't mind repeats. This system also ensures that the grocery list is exactly the same each week. In fact, they simply make grocery lists on their computers and print a bunch of them.

Other gals want diversity and variety to set their menus apart. They have a large repertoire of meals from which to choose. They keep the menu rotating enough that their families, when dining on a dish, can't remember the last time it was served. One woman I know has 365 main-dish recipes she uses each year. Her family never has a repeat meal all year. My family loves my cheesy chicken pot pie and Italian stuffed shells much too much to go for that setup, but I guess it works for her clan.

Crafting a Menu Plan

First, you need to ask yourself what amount of variety you want to have in your family's weekly meals. Here are some possible scenarios.

A one-week, a two-week, or a monthly rotation. The benefit of operating this way is you can easily make a shopping list since the menu never changes; it just rotates. The downside is that it doesn't take advantage of what items are on sale, so it can be a little more costly. If you have glazed pork loin on your rotating menu, but it isn't on sale when you shop, your food bill will be higher.

Making your menu according to the weekly grocery store flyer. This tends to be more cost effective. In this plan, you see what meats and main dish items are on sale, and then you plan your menu around them. This takes more effort on your part than the rotation menu plan. You might read several different stores' flyers, comparing the prices of meat, potatoes, and other needed ingredients. Next you'll need to make your week's menu and make out a shopping plan, taking into account which stores had what items at the best prices.

A modified freezer-cooking menu with a few from-scratch meals thrown in. This is the method that has worked for me for the past ten years or so. You set aside a chunk of time—perhaps working with a friend to double your efforts and divide the results—to put several main dishes, side dishes, and dessert items into the freezer to use on your busiest days during the month. The rest of the time you can cook as normal, using ingredients from your fridge and pantry. More on this method a little later.

Crunch-time cooking. This is where you don't even think about supper until at least 4:30. You frantically dash to the cupboard to locate three or four items that, when thrown together, could resemble something close to a family dinner. But when you realize there is no hamburger to go with your Hamburger Helper (and you recall how your family balked the last time you served them just Helper), you dash to the store for a rotisserie chicken and a bag of salad or pick up some $5 pizzas for the third time that week. Yep, that's crunch-time cooking. I've used it, but I don't recommend it.

Making a Grocery List

Do you know the perils of shopping without a list? Experts assert that you spend up to 25 percent more on such shopping trips. After planning your menu, come up with a grocery list to keep you organized and save money.

If you choose method #1, a rotating menu, you'll have an easier time of this. Lay out all your recipes, and begin to make a shopping sheet. Get out a piece of paper, go through each recipe, item by item, and write the needed ingredients on the paper along with the amounts. As you go through the recipes, notice any repeated ingredients. Perhaps your first main dish is meatloaf. Your recipe calls for ground beef, ketchup, saltines, onions, green pepper, crushed garlic, and eggs. Write down these ingredients, keeping a somewhat logical order to them. Perhaps you'll list meats on the top of the page, veggies and fruits in the middle, and other items on the bottom. Be sure that after each item you write how much of it is needed. Perhaps after ground beef, you'll put two hash marks representing two pounds, the amount your meatloaf calls for. For onion and green pepper you'll put hash marks that represent one-half cup each (which is approximately one-half of a medium onion or one whole medium green pepper). For crushed garlic, you'll put one mark per teaspoon.

After doing this exercise with a few more main dishes, you come to lasagna. This recipe also calls for ground beef, onion, green pepper, and garlic. Instead of listing these over again, add the amounts needed to the already listed item. When all the recipes have been logged in, add up the various components. Now you know just how many pounds of potatoes, chicken, and ground beef you need and also how many cans of tomatoes, mushrooms, etc. Do this for any side dishes and desserts. And don't forget lunches. List what you need to buy for the kids' lunches and also breakfast items.

The result will be your rotating-menu shopping list. Now transfer all your items and amounts to a printed grocery list (use the sample list on pages 227 and 229 or come up with your own) that follows your store's grocery aisles to help ensure you won't need to keep running back and forth across the store to retrieve items you missed. You can now add other items you need such as paper goods, beauty products, and other nonfood items. Take note the next time you visit your local supermarket of its exact layout. Some stores even have this information available in printed form at customer service.

If you chose method #2, making your menu from the weekly sale flyer, you'll need to make a new grocery list each week. Follow the same steps laid out for method #1. You may want to use a highlighter or two to indicate which stores you want to purchase ingredients at to get the best prices. When I handled my grocery shopping this way, I shopped at two different stores. I highlighted the items from one store and left the others unhighlighted.

If you choose method #3, freezer cooking with some from-scratch meals each week, you'll want to use method #1 or #2 to prepare those from-scratch meals. Will you have a few regular recipes to round out your week? Or will you make them using the best sale items that week? Decide and proceed accordingly.

For method #4, crunch-time cooking, no advanced preparation is needed. It can work in the short-term but will cost you the most money. Try as you might, you'll still need to operate this way occasionally. The key is *occasionally!* That does not mean three to four times a week. And when it comes to making a list, crunch-time cooking is the simplest yet. You don't even need a list. You only need three things: directions to the nearest grocery store, a phone book opened to the carry-out restaurant section, and a lot of cash!

Printed Grocery List

No matter which method you use, one list-making idea that has worked wonders for me, can save you time and money, and train your family in this area, is to have a printed grocery list posted on the fridge at all times. Years ago, between babies #1 and #2, I printed a grocery list of the foods, paper products, heath and beauty aids, and household products I purchased on a regular basis. I listed these items in the order I normally find them at my local grocery store.

Next, I trained all my family members who could read to help mom make the grocery list each week. When anyone used the last bit of something—the final squirt of mustard, the last egg in a dozen, or the final teaspoon of sugar—he or she would walk over to the list and circle that item. When we first began this routine, Mackenzie would pride herself on announcing to me, "Mom, we need more ketchup. But don't worry. I already circled it." It also worked well for my husband. When he arrived home in the middle of the night after work, he could dump the last few tablespoons of chocolate chips into the peanut-butter jar, dig in deep with a spoon, and then grab a crayon and circle those two items with an unsteady hand so I would think one of the kids polished them off.

Because we don't eat the same meals each week and this list mostly laid out the regular items we keep on hand, I knew I'd have other items to add. So I left blank space at the end of each section to jot items down in their proper location and keep my logical order.

Your family probably will have a list that looks different from mine. We have regular items that are considered "must have on hand" at our house that might puzzle you, such as light cherry-pie filling. It's a major ingredient in the low-fat, black-forest sheet cake I like to make often.

I have included a sample generic printed list in the appendix on pages 227 and 229 to serve as an example. Your best bet is to take the time to make up a list that will be unique to your family. Remember to leave space at the end of each section to jot down items for the particular recipes you'll be making.

Once your family has gotten the hang of this system, you'll be halfway done making out your shopping list. Grab your sheet off the fridge. Sit down and add any other food items you'll need according to your menu plan. Remember to look at each section and write down other purchases you might need to make. Do you need paper towels, shampoo, dog food? Is your supply of water-softener salt running low? How about toothpaste? If there are stores other than the supermarket you need to run to, you may find it helpful to flip over your list and jot the store and purchases on the reverse side. Such stores might include the drugstore to pick up a prescription or the dry cleaners to drop off or pick up clothes. Now you are ready to hit the road—almost.

Checking It Twice

Before stepping out the door and being on your merry way, you need to take a quick inventory of what you have on hand to avoid buying duplicates. To avoid letting your pantry get to the Old Mother Hubbard stage, once you have your list in hand, check your pantry and fridge. Do you already have the shredded cheese for the tacos? Got a can of cream-of-something soup you can dump into the casserole? Plenty of oats and chocolate chips for your famous cookies, which you plan to make for the baseball team? Then don't put those items on the list in the first place (takes more brain function to do it that way!) or, after your list is made, "go shopping" in your own kitchen and cross off the items you don't need to buy. This way, when you're standing in the grocery store aisle and you see your list includes a jar of peach jam for your glazed chicken, you won't need to stare at the shelf wondering, *Hmmm…don't I already have a jar of this at home? If I buy it now when it isn't on sale and I don't have a coupon and then get home and find out I do have a jar, I'll kick myself. On the other hand, if I don't get it and then find out I was mistaken about already having it, I'll have to run back to the store or change what I was planning to serve.*

Taking inventory before you go prevents such scenarios, thereby saving both time and money. So check your pantry, fridge, and freezer before trekking off. If you are someone who stocks a lot in your freezer, here's another tip: Purchase a magnetic write on/wipe off board and hang it on the freezer door. Post what items are in your deep freeze, along with the quantities. Perhaps your board will list the types of frozen vegetables you use, such as corn, green beans, and broccoli. After each veggie, place a number telling you how many bags are in there. Then, when you retrieve a bag for dinner, change the number to reflect how many bags are left. It works well for all freezer items: cans of orange juice, pounds of ground beef, bags of frozen steak fries, etc. Or make up a freezer list on your computer that you can run off every so often. Leave blanks after the entries to list the quantities on hand.

Developing a "Ma Ingalls" Mentality

Before we move on to cooking the foods we plan and shop for, I want to address a component of food preparation that has gone by the wayside in most homes today: cooking from scratch.

When Mackenzie was in her Laura Ingalls Wilder stage, I learned many things from reading about the life of this wise woman. I've already mentioned following her advice to divide tasks up over the days of the week. Simple, but so helpful! There was another practice that struck me as I read about Ma all those lazy afternoons before naptime. She was a woman who could whip up anything from scratch. Think about it!

The word pictures Laura paints of the pickle preserves, the sparkling jars of homemade jam, the smell of potatoes boiling and fresh bread baking, and apple pies cooling on the table, seem so Norman Rockwell. But where did all these wonderful foodstuffs come from? Did she trot off to the supermarket to pick up premade creations? Of course not. What she bought can be summed up in one much-forgotten word in our society when it comes to food shopping: *staples*.

I daresay that most 20-, 30-, and 40-something moms haven't a clue when it comes to buying staples and cooking from scratch. Once when I ran out of flour, I attempted to borrow some from a neighbor. When she told me she didn't have any, I chimed in, "Oh, you out too?" "Oh no," she replied. "I haven't ever bought flour."

This gal had been married and a mother for more than a decade. She had made cakes, muffins, and cookies. However, she told me she never had a need to buy a bag of flour because she only made cakes from mixes and baked cookies from refrigerated cookie dough.

But good ol' Ma Ingalls was just the opposite. She was very inventive with whatever she had on hand. One time she even made an apple pie for Pa out of green pumpkins soaked in lemon juice because she didn't have any apples on hand. Pa didn't even notice, and in fact, he said it was the best apple pie he'd ever eaten.

Think about it: She only had three places to "shop." She had the family garden for produce. She had the animals—a cow for milk; meat from the game Pa shot, including rabbit, squirrel, and deer; and the occasional pig, cow, and chicken they butchered. And she had Olsen's General Store. But what did she buy there on her excursions to town? Some potato chips for Pa and fruit bites and pricey juice boxes for the girls? Nope. She bought staples: flour, sugar, salt, cocoa powder.

From staples we can make many delicious, low-cost, and healthy dishes. But it isn't easy. No whipping open a package when you return home from the store. You'll have many ingredients in your grocery sacks, but few finished products. In fact, a good indication that you've had a successful shopping trip is if you return home, put it all away, and declare, "There's nothing to eat!" That's because you need to *make* something to eat.

If only we could see the money we've wasted over the years by buying ready-made food. We would cry! Yes, there are times we need to buy packaged fare, but let's face it—for the most part we buy it because we're either lazy or unorganized. And it's draining our bank accounts.

From staples you can make an array of entrees, side dishes, and desserts. "Who has the time?" you ask. I've found that when I say that, what I really mean is I don't want to make the time.

If a friend calls and wants to chat, do you stop and talk for twenty minutes or so? That's about how long it takes to whip up a batch of homemade muffins, cookies, or granola. We greatly overestimate how long it takes to cook from scratch. And in this case, time is money. We can reduce our grocery bills if we begin to cook and bake rather than buy ready-made foods. The transition won't happen overnight, but you can begin now to make small changes toward being a more frugal shopper and cook.

For premade items that you'll buy, compare prices. Comparison shopping is much easier now with unit pricing displayed on those stickers on the side of the shelf. These tell you just how much that particular item costs per pound, per ounce, or per 100. So make it a habit to compare prices. Realize that the item you have a coupon for isn't always the best deal, so don't buy an item just because you have a coupon. Leave the coupon on the store shelf as a blessing to the next person.

My mother-in-law is famous for telling her kids and grandkids, "You are the sum of your choices." Never has that been truer than at the grocery store. So as you make your menu and resulting shopping list, think simple, develop a Ma Ingalls mentality, and make it yourself!

Thinking Outside the Shopping Cart

Here are some pointers to help you break out of your old shopping routine and add order and a little pocket change to your life.

Change what store you go to. Shopping at budget stores can cut your grocery bill by up to one-third. They have your basic staples, their own store's brand of many convenience foods if you still want to buy them, and a limited selection of meats, dairy, and produce. You won't find out-of-the-ordinary items. You might even need a specialty grocery store for those.

Buy in bulk, but only if you'll use it all, can freeze some, or can split it with a friend. It makes no sense to purchase a big box of something that goes bad before you use it all.

Do your exercises. The food industry uses many tricks to get you to buy things. A huge one is their strategy to get the average shopper, a five-foot-six female, to buy the most expensive items. That's why, in the baking aisle, for example, the most costly cake and muffin mixes are at eye level. The cheaper off-brand and bargain-brand mixes are up high or down low. So reach up or stoop down to grab the savings.

Buy a fizz keeper. This is a device that keeps the bubbly in your soda. You give it a few pumps, and you're good to go. That way you can buy a large bottle rather than individual cans. You can enjoy the savings and the soda because it won't go flat before it's all consumed.

Buy perishable items in season and freeze or can them for future use. My mother did this all the time and taught me how as a young bride. Not only is it a healthy practice, but when your four-year-old wants corn on the cob for his cowboy birthday in the middle of January, you won't need to take a second mortgage on the house to buy some. Farmers markets are fabulous. You can buy fruits and vegetables at reasonable prices. Also, put the word out to your friends who have gardens. Inform them you'd be happy to pick their excess. Also, if freezing and canning is new to you, buy a comprehensive how-to guide. The *Ball Blue Book of Preserving* by Alltrista Consumer Products and *Stocking Up* by Carol Hupping are my favorites. Both were given to me by my mom and are now food spattered and well loved.

Avoid foods that are packaged together that can be purchased separate for less. You pay big bucks for the added handiness of premeasured packaged foods. So sprinkle your own granola on yogurt. Toss some raisins and walnuts on your oatmeal. You can even make up your own flavored oatmeal packets using plastic sandwich bags. Measure out one serving of instant oatmeal from a large canister and add dried fruits, nuts, cinnamon, and sugar. In the morning, follow original cooking directions.

Don't pay the store to put the finishing touches on your food. Don't buy cut produce unless there's a good reason to do so. You can "pay" your child to help you with this task. Find what kid-pleasing snacks are on sale that week, and buy one of those treats to give as a reward. However, your child will need to clean and cut produce like carrots and celery and place them in plastic zip bags when you return home. When finished, he or she gets "paid" with the purchased treat.

Always check for markdowns. Look for special orange or yellow stickers noting reductions taken on close-to-expiration food items. I know my local market marks meat and dairy items down at 5:00 P.M. and even further after 9:00 P.M. If I'm in town, I swing by to see what has been reduced. I've gotten salmon, normally $5.99 a pound for a mere $.99 a pound! Milk is usually good three days past the expiration date if it hasn't been opened. If you store dairy cartons like sour cream and ricotta cheese upside down, they keep up to two weeks longer.

What Works for Me

Carmen Peterson, Illinois

When it comes to cooking, I have five very willing and helpful sets of hands. I started letting the kids take one day a month to help me in the kitchen. It's not only their special day to help, but they get to pick the meal as well. We use the day that their birthday is on to be their day of the month. So Angel, who was born on the third, gets her special day on the third of each month.

I put their names on the calendar in big bold letters stating it's their day to help cook. This has given me a chance to have one-on-one time with each child and teach them about cooking. We cover things like cooking terms and ingredients. My five-year-old son, who loves lasagna and often picks that as his meal, can put together a mean lasagna and tell you what it means to boil water, thaw out hamburger, and more!

What Works for Me

Marybeth Whalen, North Carolina

Do you struggle to make lunch interesting beyond the normal PB&J? I have found it's easy to vary your lunches if you keep a running list of alternatives to sandwiches. Here are some ideas that are inexpensive and quick.

- Breakfast for lunch, which might be scrambled eggs

with canned biscuits or cinnamon rolls, boiled eggs with fruit and cheese, cinnamon toast with bacon, or frozen biscuits made into sausage-and-egg sandwiches.

- Egg-salad on Wheat Thins.

- Microwave egg sandwich: Spray a small bowl with a bit of cooking spray. Crack an egg into the bowl and microwave it for one minute. Serve on an English muffin topped with a slice of deli ham.

- Jarred pasta sauce served over pasta twists.

- Pasta twists mixed with Italian dressing and leftover grilled chicken. You can add broccoli, sliced tomatoes, black olives—whatever you like—to make a wonderful chilled pasta salad.

- Boxed macaroni and cheese served with sliced apples or applesauce.

- Pita pockets stuffed with deli meat and packaged shredded lettuce. Pour a bit of your favorite salad dressing on for flavor.

- Baked potatoes topped with shredded cheese, bacon bits, butter, and sour cream. Let the kids create their own.

- Chef salad made with bagged greens, chopped boiled eggs, deli meat, bacon bits, and any other veggies you like.

- Soup with crackers—oyster crackers or goldfish are fun choices.

- Frozen pizzas.

- Soft tortillas sprinkled with shredded cheese and cooked in the microwave for a few seconds. Dip into ranch dressing, sour cream, or salsa. Serve with packaged baby carrots and ranch dressing.

• • • • • • • **From the Heart of a Kid** • • • • • • • •

Hey, Mom! Does your snack menu consist of Doritos, candy bars, and other assorted junk foods? Do you think your kids won't eat healthy foods? Here are some quick and delicious healthy snacks that your kids will have fun making and eating.

- Instead of having just a piece of fruit, make it fun. Cut up a bunch of fruit and thread it on a bamboo skewer. Introduce them to out-of-the-ordinary fruits like mango, pineapple, kiwi, and Asian pear—my favorite!

- If your kids are like my baby brother and will eat *anything* dunked in ranch dip, try washed and cut veggies. I'm not just talkin' carrots and celery. We love red, orange, and yellow peppers (loaded with vitamin C, by the way), broccoli, cauliflower, and even whole mushrooms.

- Invest in an apple peeler/corer/slicer. When we were younger, we didn't always get excited about eating a normal apple. But when mom used that cool machine, it would make them come out peeled and looking like a Slinky. We called them "doingy" apples, and we *would* eat those and beg for more.

- Ants on a log. For a twist on this celery snack, use low-fat cream cheese with dried cherries or cranberries or a kid favorite: marshmallow cream with chocolate chips or M&M's (come on, it's healthy—it's on celery!).

- Spear chunks of assorted cheeses with pretzel sticks.

- Yogurt parfaits are great for getting your children to eat more fruits and dairy. Layer low-fat yogurt and their favorite fruits in fancy, clear cups, and sprinkle granola on top.

☺ Mackenzie

NOW YOU'RE COOKIN'!

How are you doing, Mom? Did you take inventory of what food-stuffs you had on hand before going shopping? Have you made a family-pleasing menu plan? Made a list and checked it twice? Purchased, paid for, and lugged home all those grocery items? Then you're ready to cook!

Cooking, like so many other areas we have addressed thus far, is best handled with a plan in mind. Taking the crunch-time approach—simply walking to the fridge or pantry and trying to find something to whip up—works occasionally, but it isn't the best way to ensure culinary success. Finding a routine or rhythm that works for you and fits your schedule and lifestyle will be the key to cooking with relative ease. Here are a few ideas to consider.

- Invest in a slow cooker and a few good slow-cooker cookbooks. So many yummy meals can be assembled the night before and then popped into the slow cooker the next day. Your supper cooks while you go about your day. I've listed my favorite cookbooks at the end of this chapter.

- Plan your meals in logical order. If you're going to have both tacos and Sloppy Joes for dinner choices, have them one or two days apart and brown enough ground beef for both meals at the same time. Take out half the meat for the Sloppy Joes, and mix it with the sauce ingredients. Leave the rest in the pan and continue making the tacos, adding the necessary spices. If you're going to make a baked-chicken dish and you're pretty sure you'll have some poultry left over, plan to make homemade chicken noodle soup or chicken enchiladas the next night.

- Chop and freeze leftover meat. Label it well and keep track of what you have in the freezer so you can use it up before too long (see my favorite freezer guides listed in chapter 8).

- Try freezer cooking to free up some time during the week. I heartily recommend it! I have been doing this for over a decade, and it fits our lifestyle well. It saves time, money, and work. Why get out a pan, brown a pound of something, wash the pan, and put it away 30 times a month? It makes more sense to cook the meat for the entire month all at once, wash the pans, and put them away. Or why buy shredded cheese in the more expensive smaller bag? If you bought a huge bag from the warehouse store, froze portions, and used all of it, you'd pay much less per pound. Quantity cooking and freezing ahead makes sense on many fronts.

Quantity Cooking

I know many women roll their eyes when they hear the concept of "once a month" cooking. They envision casseroles with "cream of something" soup glopped on top of noodles. That's not what I'm talking about at all.

A few years back I became friends with one of the founders of the "30 Day Gourmet" freezer manual and Web site (www.30daygourmet. com). I bought their freezer manual, and my homemaking life was forever changed. You see, all the meals are appetizing and family friendly. When making larger quantities of any of the recipes, the numbers have already been crunched for you. So when tripling a meal, you needn't strain your brain, pondering, *Now what is four times 3 and 2/3 cups?* In addition to main dishes, there are sides, breads and muffins, desserts, snacks, and even breakfast sandwiches.

There are dozens of wonderful freezer cookbooks. And there are just as many ways to freezer cook. One idea: When making a main dish for supper, make two and freeze one for later. Make a half-dozen or so main dishes on Saturday mornings for your family to eat on the craziest nights that month.

For even more efficiency, start a cooking co-op. Four to six in a co-op group is ideal. Assign a different chosen dish or two to each participant. Each person makes their dishes, divides them so each co-op member gets one family-sized dinner portion, and freezes them. Finally you all get together and trade. Each woman returns home with meals for a week or more. You have a fantastic variety, but each of you only had to make one or two dishes. Assembling multiples of one type of entree is a snap compared to making several different kinds. If you'd like more information on starting a freezer cooking co-op, check out www.cookingamongfriends.com. Most all freezer cookbooks will help you with the basics, such as what to freeze and what not to freeze, how to utilize space by using one- and two-gallon bags, frozen flat, and what to do if space is limited.

I cook and freeze ahead another way. I find it much easier to work when I am doing it alongside someone else. I have had the most success when following the buddy system. Here's how it works.

Select some favorite chicken, beef, pork, pasta, or vegetarian meals. Have a friend do the same. Meet to plan your menu and grocery lists, and then shop separately. Keep good records of what you spend so the two of you can settle up.

On assembly day get the children involved in something else that will keep them out of the kitchen. If they are little, cook on a Saturday when the dads can hang with the kids or hire a sitter to occupy them. Arrive with your ground meats already browned and any other meats previously cooked in a slow cooker or roaster the day before. Bring the rest of the needed ingredients and assemble away! When I started doing this over a decade ago, I'd return home with 10 or 12 meals. The last time I did it, I had over 90! I also had some breakfast sandwiches, bread-machine mixes, and desserts.

Wait! Don't pick up the phone and try to convince a girlfriend that the two of you must make a hundred meals for each of your families by the day after tomorrow. Make plans to do this in a week or two. Start with five or ten meals apiece. From there you can branch out if you choose to: increase the number of meals or add side dishes, desserts, muffins, or simple breakfast foods.

Another aspect of freezer cooking that I love is being ready to take a meal to a family with a new baby, a family that has experienced a tragedy, or someone in need. Now when you get the phone call or hear through the grapevine about a person in need of a meal, you won't have to fret about all the work it will take to pull off such a feat. You can simply pull a meal out of your freezer. Try to have one such standby meal ready on a consistent basis. Maybe it will be a pan of lasagna, a vegetable side dish, and a frozen pie or cake. If you don't use up the meal for such a situation, your family can always eat it.

The Family Plan

Every family will have a different plan for how they'd like mealtime to work at their homes. You'll have your family favorites, your special snack-time traditions, and other regulars that round out your menu. I have included some recipes in the appendix for you to try. For the remainder of this chapter, we'll focus on function. We'll brainstorm some shortcuts. We'll invent some ways to make food prep and clean-up easier. And we'll even take a look at kids in the kitchen. We can actually train them at a young age to help!

Kitchen Shortcuts

Try building these shortcuts into your cooking routine. They will save you time and effort.

- Get a jump on cooking meat. Brown several pounds of ground beef at a time. Cool and divide into several freezer bags, label, and freeze. Make sure your portions make sense. If your favorite chili recipe calls for two pounds of ground beef, freeze your meat in this portion. Note that one pound of raw ground beef equals 2½ cups when cooked. You can also add taco seasoning or Sloppy Joe sauce before freezing.

- Take it up a notch or two. While browning beef, add onions, garlic, and green peppers. Use this in any recipe that calls for these items such as chili, spaghetti sauce, or goulash.

- Chop leftover chicken and turkey and freeze in labeled bags. Later, turn these into soups, casseroles, or tacos. You'll be one step closer to dinner.

- Celery, onions, and green and red peppers need not be blanched (boiled for a minute) before freezing. Chop up a bunch and store in freezer bags for up to one year. It will save time as you need only get out what you need to add to your recipe.

- To have healthy snacks at your fingertips, peel and cut up carrots, celery, cucumbers, and peppers. Store them in plastic bags in the fridge. They can be easily grabbed and coupled with a low-fat ranch dip or dressing for a nutritious snack.

- When you get to the bottom of the box of crackers or croutons, pour the crumbs into a plastic bag. Add to meatloaf and meatballs or use as a coating for chicken.

- Make your own frozen dinners. Purchase some compartmentalized microwave containers with lids. Place your main dish, sides, and dessert in the containers' compartments, and seal tightly with the lid. Store up to one month in the freezer. For lunch on the go or on busy nights, reheat with the lid slightly ajar.

- For a quick, sweet treat, freeze cookie-size balls of your favorite cookie dough on a cookie sheet for an hour or two. Transfer to a plastic zipper bag and freeze. To bake, simply add a minute or two to the original directions.

Cleanup in Aisle Nine

As moms, sometimes our biggest headache isn't deciding what we'll serve or even preparing the meal itself. It's the dreaded cleanup. To keep this chore less bothersome, try:

- Line pans with foil or parchment paper to cut cleanup time. While foil works great for tasks like broiling a pan of nachos, remember that tomato-based foods (like lasagna) can eat through foil.

- Begin your cleanup and storage of leftovers at the table rather than having everyone carry their plates to the kitchen and then trying to make sense of it all. Scrape plates and condense leftovers right at the table. Have containers nearby to place leftovers in to freeze or for lunch the next day. Stack the scraped dishes. Corral the cups. Place all the condiments at one end of the table to be transported to the fridge. You may not want to follow this routine when entertaining.

- If you must hand-wash dishes, think in logical order. Wash less-soiled items like glassware first, then silverware, slightly dirty plates, and bowls. End with the pots and pans and messy serving dishes. You won't need to change the water as often this way.

- Realize that items with eggs, such as the skillet from scrambled eggs, will wash best in cold water. Hot water bakes the eggs on further.

- Have the sink full of hot, soapy water, and soak any pans with baked-on messes while you eat your meal.

- When cleaning up the table and floor underneath, remember that dirt follows gravity. Wipe the table before you sweep. Better yet, have a child wipe the table and then another one sweep. You put your feet up!

Beyond the Cereal Bowl

One of the most expensive items, when figured by the pound, is dry breakfast cereal. While my brood loves their Cap'n Crunch's Peanut Butter Crunch as much as the neighbors down the street cherish their Cheerios, we plan variety into our morning routine, which can save us money as well. Sound too difficult? Try these easy breakfast favorites.

- Slow-cooker oatmeal. Place 6 cups of water, 3 cups of old-fashioned rolled oats (not quick oats), and a dash of salt in the slow cooker just before bedtime. Cover and cook on low for 6 to 8 hours. Family members can customize their bowls in the morning by adding: butter, brown sugar, raisins, cinnamon, dried cherries or cranberries, strawberry jam, sliced bananas, walnuts, peanut butter, maple syrup.

- Shredded Wheat biscuits—my husband's childhood

favorite. Pour a little boiling water over a couple of large biscuits in a bowl. Let it sit a minute, and then drain. Top with butter, brown sugar, maple syrup, and peanut butter. Yum! A great way to sneak fiber into your kids' diets.

- Breakfast sandwiches (from www.30daygourmet .com). Make a large batch and freeze for busy days. Bake homemade buttermilk or whole-grain biscuits until lightly golden, but *not* overdone. (For a short-cut, use the ready-made, whack-open kind.) Cool and split. Place within the two halves a well-cooked egg and a meat (a slice or two of cooked bacon, a cooked sausage patty, or a portion of ham or Canadian bacon). You can add a slice of cheese as well. Wrap each sandwich tightly in foil, label, and freeze. To cook, place sandwiches, thawed and still wrapped in foil, in the oven and warm for 20 to 25 minutes at 400 degrees. Or wrap one in a damp paper towel and microwave on high for a minute. You can also make these healthier by using low-fat cheese, egg substitute, and meatless sausage patties.

- Make a batch of bran, banana nut, or other muffin batter. Cover and place in the refrigerator overnight. In the morning, bake the muffins up fresh and serve with cut-up fruit.

- Make your favorite waffles or pancakes, doubling the recipe. To freeze leftovers, cool and place between pieces of wax paper. Wrap tightly in foil and freeze. Reheat in the toaster or microwave.

Make-Ahead Mixes

Setting aside some time either alone or with friends to create any of the following mixes will save you time on a busy day. Be sure to have the final instructions handy, listing the fresh ingredients you'll add the day you make the finished product. You can even write simpler instructions on a note card and tuck it into the bag. These first two mixes are from my friend Kelly Hovermale and are regular staples at our house.

Buttermilk Pancake Mix

Combine the following dry ingredients, mixing well, then place in a container with a tight-fitting lid and store in freezer or fridge.

Mix
9 cups whole-wheat pastry flour or white whole-wheat flour
2¼ teaspoons salt
2 tablespoons baking soda

Fresh ingredients
3 eggs
3 cups buttermilk
oil

To make pancakes: Beat 3 eggs in a large bowl. Add 3 cups buttermilk, mixing well. Whisk in 3 cups plus 1 tablespoon of dry mix until blended. Cook on well oiled, hot griddle until bubbly, about 2 to 3 minutes. Flip and cook 1 minute more.

Serves 6.

Whole-Grain Oat Waffle Mix

Combine the following and store in a container with a tight-fitting lid or in a large plastic bag with a zip closure. You may also split evenly into four bags for freezing, placing 1¾ cups dry mix per bag.

Mix
6 cups quick oats
2 cups whole-wheat pastry flour or white whole-wheat flour
1 tablespoon plus 1 teaspoon baking soda
1 tablespoon plus 1 teaspoon sugar
2 teaspoons salt

Fresh ingredients
2 eggs
2 cups buttermilk
2 tablespoons butter
Cooking spray

To make waffles: Whisk 2 eggs, 2 cups buttermilk, and 2 tablespoons of melted, slightly cooled butter in a bowl. Whisk in 1¾ cups dry waffle mix (or one bag if you packaged this in four individual bags). Heat your waffle iron. Coat with cooking spray. Pour batter into iron and cook according to the manufacturer's directions for your machine. Makes 8 rectangular waffles.

Serve with butter, syrup, fruit topping, whipped cream, or our favorite: natural-style peanut butter and homemade jam.

Hint: White whole-wheat flour can be found in major supermarkets. King Arthur's brand is a great one. Whole-wheat pastry flour can be found in health-food sections at the grocery stores. Better yet, invest in a flour mill and grind your own wheat. I never imagined I'd fork over the money for one, but friends who ground their own grain turned out baked goods that melted in my mouth, while mine, using purchased flour, always tasted like cardboard. So I made the leap. Using freshly ground wheat also retains the nutritional value of the grain.

Calico Cookies
Mix up a batch of these to have on hand when you'd like to make

cookies without making a big mess. Combine the ingredients thoroughly and store dry mix in a gallon freezer bag. Double or triple the recipe if you'd like and put up multiple bags for busy days.

Mix
¾ cup sugar
¾ cup firmly packed brown sugar
1¼ cups all-purpose flour
1 teaspoon baking soda
½ teaspoon salt
3 cups quick oats

Fresh ingredients
1 cup butter
2 eggs
1 teaspoon vanilla or coconut extract or orange extract
1½ cups of any combination of nuts, coconut, dried cranberries, raisins, and chips; chocolate, butterscotch, cinnnamon, white chocolate.

To make cookies: In a large bowl, cream 1 cup butter, softened. Add 2 eggs and 1 teaspoon extract, mixing well. Blend in dry mix until well incorporated. Add 1½ cups of any add-ins you want, mixing and matching if desired. Just make sure the total is 1½ cups. Try chocolate, butterscotch, peanut butter, cinnamon, white chocolate chips, chopped nuts, coconut; dried cranberries, cherries, or raisins. Vary the recipe by substituting coconut or orange extract for vanilla. Get creative! Anything goes.

Place heaping tablespoons of dough onto an ungreased cookie sheet. Bake at 375° for 9 to 11 minutes until lightly golden. Cool 3 to 5 minutes and remove.

Makes 3 to 4 dozen.

Fruit Crisp Topping

Using a pastry blender, combine the mix ingredients until crumbly. Store in a bag or container and place in freezer.

Mix (Crisp Topping)
3 cups firmly packed brown sugar
2 cups all-purpose flour
1 cup quick or old-fashioned oats
1⅓ cups butter, chilled and cut into little squares

Fresh ingredients
Cooking spray or oil to grease the pan
sliced peaches, sliced tart apples, blueberries, raspberries,
    or blackberries—fresh or frozen—or pie filling
1 cup sugar
¼ cup flour
¼ teaspoon salt

To make a crisp: Place any of the following in a greased 9 x 13-inch pan: thinly sliced peaches or tart apples, blueberries, raspberries, or blackberries (fresh or frozen). Sprinkle with 1 cup sugar mixed with ¼-cup flour and ¼ teaspoon salt. Stir slightly. Sprinkle on about half the crisp topping, saving the rest for another day.

Bake at 375 degrees until bubbly, about 30 to 40 minutes.

For an even faster shortcut, use cans of pie filling instead of fresh or frozen fruit. You'll need four cans for a 9 x 13-inch crisp.

Bread Machine Mix

Use this wonderful mix to make dough for pizza or cinnamon rolls. Or make a traditional loaf of bread. This is taken from *The Freezer Cooking Manual* by my friend Nanci Slagle of 30 Day Gourmet. It's available at www.30daygourmet.com.

Mix

Combine the following in a large bowl:

5 pounds plus 1 cup all-purpose flour

1 cup sugar or brown sugar

1 cup powdered buttermilk

1 teaspoon salt

Fresh ingredients

1 cup warm water

1 egg

2 tablespoons butter or oil

1 bag bread mix

1½ teaspoons dry yeast

Package 3½ cups of mix in six quart-size zippered bags. Put the individual bags into a larger, two-gallon zipper bag, and store in the freezer.

To make dough: Allow one bag of mix to come to room temperature. Place the fresh ingredients, along with the bread mix, in your bread machine (in the order recommended by the manufacturer).

To make bread: If you'd like to make a loaf of regular bread, set your machine to the "1½-pound loaf white bread, light crust." If you want to make pizza, calzones, or cinnamon rolls, select the "dough" setting.

I like to make breadsticks: Once the dough cycle is finished, spread the dough on a greased cookie sheet forming a large rectangle. Using a sharp knife, score the dough into sticks about an inch wide. Let dough rest, covered, at room temperature for 15 to 20 minutes. Bake at 400 degrees 8 to 12 minutes or until no longer doughy. Remove, brush with melted butter, and sprinkle with Italian spices, garlic powder, and parmesan cheese.

Using a pizza cutter, cut into bread sticks along the score marks. Dip in ranch dressing, spaghetti sauce, or olive oil.

Yum! So easy and versatile.

The Soul Food Kitchen

The kitchen is a powerful room. It can be a center of nourishment for the body and soul. It can be the place where great family memories are forged. It can be an avenue of love as we provide our husbands and children with what their bodies need to keep them going each day. But without a plan, our kitchens serve as nothing more than expensive, lonely refueling centers where family members grab a box or rip open a bag, popping something into their mouths as they head out the door to yet another activity. Yes, families do need to have meals on the run at times. But on the days when you can, craft a meal that will be healthier than the chemical- and preservative-laden ones most families eat. It will take preparation. It will take a little time. But your loved ones are worth it, aren't they?

I want my kids to grow up remembering home-cooked meals shared with the ones they love in an unhurried manner. I'm not Pollyannaish enough to believe this will happen seven nights a week, but I certainly think we can shoot for more nights than are currently happening at our houses. Let's swim against the tide of culture, ladies, and bring back the family table!

Bring Back the Family Table

My friend Michelle Weber started a wonderful tradition in her family that has evolved into a fabulous, simple teaching tool she offers for sale to families. Implementing this concept at your home will help slow down the pace, bring back the family table, and reward your kids for the positive character traits you see them developing.

The program is called "The Family Enrichment Toolkit," and it focuses on the fruit of the Spirit to develop godly character in your children. This tradition centers on a lovely, personalized "Family

Honor Plate." Family members caught exhibiting a fruit of the spirit—love, joy, peace, patience, kindness, goodness, gentleness, and self-control—will be served their dinner on the honor plate.

Here are the main components to this great family-building strategy:

1. Catch your child doing good things and making smart choices based on godly character. (Kids might catch parents too!)

2. Celebrate those good choices and behaviors (based on character and actions not "successes") by presenting the child's meal on the Family Honor Plate.

3. Connect with your family as you bring everyone together at the dinner table to eat and learn the joy of gathering, building one another up, sharing, and growing as a family.

The kit includes:

- A simple, effective program presented on an audio CD.

- A beautiful Family Honor Plate that you personalize with your family's last name.

- A "Table Thyme" set that includes 250 discussion starters and questions.

- A free membership to a curriculum-based, character-education site so parents can pull up character-specific, historical stories of those who have shown great moral fiber. Imagine having specific information to share about Albert Einstein or Abraham Lincoln being patient the evening one of your children receives the honor plate for showing patience too.

If you would like more information about this wonderful resource, go to www.FamilyEnrichmentToolkit.com.

Great Cookbooks

Main Cookbooks

- *Crazy Plates: Low-Fat Food So Good You'll Swear It's Bad for You!* by Janet and Greta Podleski. My absolute favorite low-fat cookbook (believe me—I've tried dozens). Whimsical illustrations, health hints, and foods all my family members eat without knowing they're low-fat.

- *Miserly Meals* by Jonni McCoy. A budget-conscious volume full of great recipes, slow-cooker ideas, make-ahead mixes, and kitchen tips. You'll save the price of the book in no time flat.

- *Fix-It and Forget-It* cookbooks by Phyllis Pellman Good and Dawn J. Ranck. A must-have series for slow-cooker fans. There's a basic volume, one for entertaining, and a light-cooking one, among others.

- *Church cookbooks.* These garage-sale treasures offer tried-and-true recipes that have been hits with families. I love scouring them for new ideas.

Freezer Cookbooks

- *The Freezer Cooking Manual from 30 Day Gourmet* by Nanci Slagle. A comprehensive guide with many helpful charts and hints. Available from www.30daygourmet.com.

- *Once-a-Month Cooking* by Mary-Beth Lagerborg and Mimi Wilson. Perhaps the pioneer of the cook-ahead concept. Revised and updated for today.

- *Don't Panic—Dinner's in the Freezer* by Susie Martinez, Vanda Howell, and Bonnie Garcia. Offers a good variety of make-ahead meals for busy families.

- *Cooking Among Friends* by Mary Tennant and Becki Visser, available from www.cookingamongfriends.com. Another great freezer-cooking resource. This book also walks you through setting up a freezer-swap cooking group.

What Works for Me

Marybeth Whalen, North Carolina

Here are some shortcuts that have worked well in my kitchen.

- Go bananas! Are you forever buying bananas, only to have them turn an unsightly brown color before they get eaten? While that brown color may not look appetizing, overripe bananas are wonderful to cook with. If you don't have time to deal with them at that moment, peel them, put them in a freezer bag, and toss them in your freezer for another time. I keep adding bananas to the bag until I'm ready to make smoothies, banana bread, or pancakes. When you're ready to make something, just leave them on the counter to thaw for a half hour or so.

- Don't be chicken! Do you want to cook chicken for dinner but forgot to thaw it? One quick and easy way to thaw chicken breasts is to place them in a slow cooker on high for 1 hour. They will be ready to cook lickety-split. Now you can marinate them for the grill, put them in a casserole, boil them to use in a recipe—whatever you need to do.

- Don't cry over chopped onions! One of my favorite grocery-store finds ever has been frozen chopped onions. So many recipes I use call for chopped onions, so I was forever pulling out my chopper and crying while chopping. It dirtied up an extra appliance and added a step for me. Now, I just grab a handful of chopped onions and throw it in whatever recipe I am making. Hooray!

What Works for Me

Elaine Carr, South Carolina

This tip has saved me time and headaches! It's a simple coverall. When our children were small, a friend gave me a loose-fitting, wash-and-wear kimono she sewed for me. I found that it was handy to slip over my clothes for messy jobs such as feeding the baby, cooking, and mopping. Years later when I worked away from home, I dressed for work, then slipped such a robe over my dressy outfit to wear while I prepared breakfast, lunches, and so forth.

From the Heart of a Kid

Keeping your kitchen chores organized might seem impossible with children around. However, instead of shooing your kids away, involve them in your work. I babysit the sweetest little girl I've ever met. However, when I first started to watch her, I wouldn't let her help me in the kitchen. She didn't like that. It hurt her feelings to be treated like a little kid. As soon as I changed my game plan and gave her something to do, she showed me she could be a big help while fixing dinner for her and her siblings. Give your kids some responsibilities, and they will surprise you too. Here are some easy and fun ways to involve your children in the kitchen.

• Ask them what their favorite three or four meals are, and

then make a point to have at least one of them in the next few weeks. They'll be more likely to help make something they like eating.

- Have your kids go through coupons with you. Let them pick out one coupon for something they want, and then when at the store, they find that item in the aisles. Teach them how to decide which is the better bargain: the name brand purchased with a coupon or an off-brand that may be cheaper?

- When making dinner, let them use a butter knife and cut up veggies with you. Older kids can be in charge of making one thing, such as a tossed salad, instant pudding for dessert, or cutting out biscuits to go with the meal. Remember to have them wash their hands first. Assign them tasks so they feel they are wanted and needed.

- Here's a way your kids can help you come up with your family's menu. After every new meal my mom makes, we rate it. We tell her on a scale of 1 to 10 (10 being the highest) how much we like it. If it receives a low score, she'll ask, "Well, what should I change? Was it too salty or spicy?" The next time she'll adjust the recipe. She'll also take note of what recipes were a hit with everyone but one person. Then she'll usually make that dinner on a day that person is gone to a friend's house. She doesn't always do this. We aren't allowed to be too picky.

- Train your kids to make certain recipes and keep track of them in their own "cookbook" files on a computer or in their own handwriting. I have recipes saved including shortbread, buttermilk pancakes, and peanut butter-chocolate popcorn (a recipe I invented myself).

☺ Mackenzie

10

MAINTAINING YOUR HOME'S NEW ORDER

• •

Don't fall for the myth that once you organize your home, it will stay that way forever. You know that once you have all your ducks in a row, one of your own little ducklings will be along any minute to mess them all up again. For some of you it isn't the kiddos who are the main problem. It's you and your tendency to be fast out of the starting blocks but quick to fizzle out. Even if the folks from one of those cable TV shows came to kick out your clutter, *you* would still be the one in charge of maintaining the new order. It takes diligence and occasional short work periods to keep your fowl lined up, but the results are well worth it.

You may find it strange that up until now I haven't tackled good ol' cleaning—spring and otherwise. This is on purpose. Not only is this the most revolutionary part of this whole program, but it's the one that has most effectively helped me keep organized. I saved the best for last! Also, it's difficult to begin any kind of cleaning program when your house is cluttered. So let's get down to the nitty-gritty—literally.

Speed Cleaning

Our first dwelling was a 900-square-foot ranch home. Each Saturday, it took me about two-and-a-half hours to clean. I used a plastic compartmentalized caddy to organize all my supplies—window cleaner, wood polish, all-purpose spray, and so on. I would take one cleaning product out of the carrier and walk around my entire house using it on the surfaces it was meant for. First I'd clean all the windows. Next I tackled the wood. After that, the sinks and counters. Then I'd run the sweeper and mop the hard-surfaced floors. When I finally put all the supplies back, I had walked all around my house five or six times.

But I was introduced to a wonderful concept called Speed Cleaning by Jeff Campbell and the Clean Team (www.thecleanteam.com). It so changed how and how well I clean that I can't stop talking about it!

Here is the main premise: Instead of having all your tools and solutions in a caddy on the floor, have them in an apron on your body. This way you walk the entire perimeter of your house just once, using whatever product, brush, cloth, or bottle you need. Campbell offers clever and sturdy cleaning aprons for sale on his company's Web site. They sport multiple pockets and a strong loop on each side to hold spray bottles for windows and counters. In the pockets you put sponges, dust cloths, a toothbrush, a plastic scraper, and so on. Then tucked in your back jeans pocket or in the rear of your apron string you have an ostrich-feather duster, a champion for attracting dust.

You can also go to a hardware store and buy a canvas apron used by carpenters to hold their tools and supplies. Next, sew a loop of strong cord to each side to hold your spray bottles. Very inexpensive. Ostrich-feather dusters can be purchased at local department stores. And the Clean Team offers some wonderful, 100 percent cotton cleaning cloths that are well worth the investment. However, when I was first starting out, I found that old cloth diapers and slightly worn Fruit of the Looms worked just fine too. And I have to tell you, every single item I have purchased from the Clean Team has been worth the investment dozens of times over. My favorites are the knee pads (I have hardwood and tile floors), the apron, and the Red Juice and

Blue Juice concentrates (no, you don't drink them; they're cleaning liquids).

Where the Rubber Meets the Road

Let me walk you through a typical cleaning session in a standard home. We'll begin in the kitchen. As you encounter a surface, be it the counter, a window, or appliance, pull out the needed tools and solutions and spray and wipe away. Always work from top to bottom since dust and dirt follow gravity. If you come to a grimy sink, pull out your toothbrush and scrub around that spigot. If you need some scouring powder and a sponge, grab that and scour away. When you come to a wooden surface, grab your wood cleaner and rag and go at it. If a window is before you, spray and rub until it sparkles.

Now, let's say you are in your living room and standing in front of a shelf. No need for a major clear and clean job. Grab your ostrich-feather duster from your back pocket and give that shelf a good dusting. Then bend one knee, kicking up your foot to the rear, and knock the duster against your ankle. The dust falls off the duster and into the carpet. Now get your vacuum and finish the job. Wet mopping belongs in this last step too.

You'll have a spring in your step as you think of the time you're saving and the cleaning that is getting done. It makes so much sense to be proactive in cleaning, giving items the once over before they reach the critical stage.

Using this method, my weekly housecleaning went from about 2½ hours to an average of 50 minutes. Kenzie and Mitch, ages two and five at the time, helped too. They would follow me around with old gym socks on their hands, helping me dust. I was now touching nearly every surface in my home once a week, and my house felt so clean. If you take up speed cleaning, there will still be daily occurrences that need your attention. You'll need to wipe up a spill, shine a sink, or get that splattered toothpaste off the mirror. But for the most part, your quarters will be consistently cleaner than they were before. Once a week, speed clean. It works!

Routine Solutions

Besides your weekly cleaning, as a mom you face many other routine tasks that simply must be done. The laundry isn't going to wash, dry, and fold itself no matter how hard you snap your fingers (oh, Mary Poppins, where are you now?). The fridge and freezer aren't going to clean themselves. The baseboards aren't going to magically repel dust on a regular basis so you won't have to deal with killer dust bunnies. Create routines to help you keep on top of these tasks. Schedule them on a regular basis so these areas, along with scores of others, don't get out of hand. But where to start?

First, look over the following list of tasks, and see which ones must be done at your house. Remember, not every mom will have the same areas that bug her nor will all gals have the same standards of cleanliness. I had one friend who only cleaned her fridge out every time she moved. I was assigned that lovely job once when I helped her family pack up before moving to another state. Can anyone say hazmat suit and chisel? But you know what? It never really bothered her. She would occasionally wipe up a spill or two, but other that that, she left her fridge alone. "After all," she reasoned "my husband and I are the only ones who ever see it." On the other hand, her house was devoid of clutter completely. She was a very neat housekeeper. Keeping her fridge clean just wasn't her thing.

After deciding what routines you want to build into your life, list them on your appropriate proactive plans in your "brain in a binder." Is it something you must perform daily, once a week, or less frequently? Write them down. This will remind you to do them before they get out of control.

And here's a practice that was mentioned to me twenty years ago that has helped me immensely: When performing a chore, if you don't love doing it, remind yourself why you are doing it...and embrace the "why." Pray for your husband as you iron his work uniform and whisper a thanks to God for your kids when you pick up those toys strewn about the living room for the umpteenth time. We can be grateful to have the loved ones in our lives who create the chores for us!

Laundry

Are mounds of laundry getting you down? Try this: Have a different color laundry basket in each family member's closet. And for children old enough and responsible husbands, give each one a stain remover stick and have them treat their clothes before putting them in their baskets. On laundry day, they take their baskets to the laundry room and sort their clothes into appropriate piles—whites, lights, darks, towels and sheets, and so forth. You, dear momma, will wash and dry the clothes.

After the loads are done, either put the clothes back in the proper baskets for family members to fold and put away or spread a blanket on the floor, dump all the laundry on it, and play Friday-night find-and-fold. Family members retrieve their clothes, fold them, and put them away while you watch a video and have pizza or popcorn. You know, don't you, that even three-year-olds can learn to put away their clothes? Many of us have kids who do too little because we are moms who do too much.

I admit that sometimes I still fold the boys' clothes if they're running behind (I hate laundry sitting around). But for the most part it's every person for him- or herself. I really want my boys and my girl to know how to do laundry when they grow up and leave home. (I hope this scores me bonus points with my daughters-in-law and son-in-law someday.) Once you decide what routine you'll try, write *Laundry* on the appropriate days on your proactive plan. Be flexible. Your laundry schedule may have to change due to the sports seasons of your kids.

Toy Room

If you're a mom of young children, there are bound to be toys strewn about your home sometimes. Do you have a plan for housing all these playthings, or do they end up floating from room to room and making you blow your stack as you step on yet another Lego or Mega Blok in the middle of the night? (Ouch!) Think through the following:

- Will you allow the kids to have toys in their bedrooms or will you designate another location, say, the basement, family room, or spare room to act as a "toy room"?

- How will you keep the toys organized? Bins, baskets, cubbyholes, or shelving units?

- How will you train the kids to learn where all their toys go and put them there? I like the concept of teaching kids that all their toys have proper homes. Then, when they know where their playthings "live," you can ask them at pick-up time to take their toys and put them back where they live. My friend Sharon drew pictures and wrote words on labels on the sides of her kids' plastic toy bins and totes. She even did this on their dresser drawers. Her kids had a visual reminder for where their belongings belonged. Novel idea, right? It works well because you don't have to repeat cleanup requests.

To keep your young children's interest and prevent them from being bored, consider rotating toys. Many seasoned moms suggested this to me when our oldest was just a tot, and it's a fabulous idea. Don't put out all their toys—only about half of them. Periodically snatch some of them and replace them with others from your secret stash. Because they haven't played with them for a while, they will be fresh and new and exciting to your kids. Be sure to store the "temporarily out of service" toys in black garbage bags or dark plastic totes so they won't be spotted by little eyes.

Also, consider instituting a system to keep stray toys from wandering about your house. When a "drop and switch" kid plays with something for a short while, decides to switch gears (and toys), and happily trots off, leaving the abandoned toy behind, what's a mom to do?

Set up a "Junk Jail," that's what! Anytime you find an out-of-place toy, you'll kindly ask its owner to return it to its proper dwelling place. If after a reasonable amount of time this hasn't happened, confiscate the item and transport it to the Junk Jail. A fine must be paid to retrieve the toy. Decide what would be appropriate for each child. For younger kids, maybe the offense results in twenty-four hours without the toy. For older kids, they may need to post bond to the tune of a few quarters or even more in order to get their item back. Whatever you decide, serve as the parental warden and stick to your guns.

Once you have your toy-storage system set up, write "straighten toy room" on your (or your kids') daily, weekly, or monthly proactive plan—as often as you want to perform this task. And don't do it by yourself, Mom. Kids can straighten up their toy room too.

Spring Cleaning

In my mother's and grandmother's days, spring cleaning was a regular part of a homemaker's life. Without fail, each spring women would tackle tasks that needed to be done for deep-cleaning. Today many moms have no such practice. Maybe we should take a cue from our ancestors and resurrect the art of spring cleaning? You may even want to call an Amazon Women meeting to help each other muscle through difficult spring-cleaning jobs. Husbands can watch the children and dine on pizza and pop; the Amazon Women can dine on chocolate and cappuccinos as they tackle household chores.

And think out of the bucket. Don't feel that spring cleaning needs to be done all at once, yearly, or only in the spring. If you'd like to handle it that way, go right ahead. But I find that dividing up chores over the entire year and placing them in my proactive plan in my "brain in a binder" works better for me. Tackle them in the most logical time of the year for you. Clean out the garage during a warm month, wash walls and woodwork during a colder time of year, etc. Here are some possible tasks to tackle once a year, if not more:

- Washing walls.
- Cleaning woodwork with oil soap or another such cleanser.

- Shampooing carpets.

- Stripping or rewaxing old floors.

- Washing windows, outside as well as in.

- Weeding through the medicine cabinet, tossing outdated items.

- Cleaning and organizing the garage and basement storage areas.

- Sorting through old paint cans and harmful chemicals, properly disposing of any unwanted ones.

- Cleaning and reorganizing the pantry.

- Cleaning the coils behind or under the refrigerator (helps the fridge be more energy efficient).

- Changing the filters in the furnace.

By breaking down major cleaning projects into smaller jobs, you won't feel so overwhelmed. The key is seeing that these tasks are done. When an area hasn't seen a damp cloth in years, it's discouraging to tackle the situation. By having a plan, hopefully these chores won't seem so unpleasant.

Seasons of Change

By now I'm sure it has occurred to you that there will be various seasons of motherhood. Your kids will grow up and have different needs materially and emotionally than they do today. In addition to the big changes that take place over the long haul as our children (and we) age, there are changes happening every month and season of the year. Kids outgrow their clothing and lose interest in some of their toys and books. It's summer and you need bug spray, sunscreen, and water toys located in a handy spot. One of your children starts a new sport, a part-time job, or moves to a new school. Do you handle the changes that happen year to year and season to season seamlessly and in an organized fashion? Write down what needs to be done. Here are some questions to ponder every so often at your house. Record them in your "brain in a binder," write them in your planner, and on your calendar. Send yourself a regular e-mail reminder. Anything! Just be sure to visit these issues two or three times a year as you adjust to the changing times.

- Have you sorted through the kids' clothing lately? What have they outgrown or no longer like or wear? What will you do with these items? Put them in storage for a younger sibling? Hand them down to another family? Donate to charity or place in a garage sale? Do you need to rotate their clothes due to the change in season? Have the kids help you with this task. Don't do it for them.

- Ask yourself the same questions with regard to outerwear—coats, gloves, hats, etc. Will you need to put these items away and get out the summer stuff—bug spray, sunscreen, water wings? Make the needed switches.

- How about your kids' rooms? Have they outgrown their rooms' décor? Time for a little sprucing up? A *Clifford the Big Red Dog* sheet set might not be great for your teenage son's new manly self-image. Plan ahead and look for appropriate items at good prices. Perhaps the nursery needs to be turned into a little girl's room. With a fresh coat of paint and a little ingenuity, a room can take on a whole new atmosphere! (And it lets our kids know we think they are worth the effort.)

- Don't forget the seasonal changes related to your children's sports and activities. Do you need to hang up the ice skates in the garage and get out the baseball gear? Is it time to pack away the soccer gear or retire the hunting clothes? Put the items needed for the current season in a handy place. Put the items that the family won't need for a while in storage.

- And what about those craft and art projects created by your children? Now here's a dilemma. You can't possibly keep them all, but you don't want to hurt your children's feelings by tossing them into the trash. Instead, display them for a period of time. Then, as often as you'd like (the end of the school year might be good), get out all the projects and have the kids set up an art gallery in the living room. Make a video of the kids describing their projects—where they made them, what materials they used, etc. Save the video, and add to it each year. As for the projects, let the kids choose two or three favorites, and store them away. Give the rest away to grandparents, a nursing home, or the children's ward at a hospital.

Holidays and Holy Days

Do you have a workable plan for staying organized when it comes to special occasions? Here are some ideas. If they work well for you, build them into your regular routine.

Set up a general store. I got this great idea from my mother-in-law. My husband tells how, as a child, he'd "purchase" something from his mom's "general store" to give to a sibling or friend for a birthday or at Christmas. The concept is simple: Purchase items on clearance that make good gifts for your children's friends. I also keep little gifts for my friends and acquaintances in my general store. When someone has a birthday, the gifts are close at hand and available! I keep my general store products in a few non-see-through plastic lidded bins in our basement.

Keep holiday decorations together in a bin in storage. Check markdown bins once a particular holiday passes to purchase on-sale items for next year. For example, purchase Easter-egg dyeing kits on the Monday after Easter or buy patriotic plates and napkins for your next Fourth of July get-together just after the holiday. If you think a year ahead, you can get these supplies at half off or more.

Transfer birthday and anniversary dates onto your new calendar. Do this on January 1. If you want to be reminded via e-mail, visit www. birthdayalarm.com and set up personal reminders for the year. This site also offers clever e-cards.

Organize Christmas. There is nothing more unnerving to some moms than Christmas. While it's a sweet time of year to lavish love on our families and friends, it also can become a stressful time with the flurry of activities and added responsibilities a mom winds up having on her plate. Several years ago I set up a holiday binder notebook (*no,* I don't have stock in a binder company. I just find them wonderful tools for moms). Here's what you'll need:

- One-inch three-ring binder. I buy the kind that has a clear front so I can slip in a picture of my kids under our tree and a Bible verse about the first Christmas.
- Three-hole-punched plastic pocket with Velcro closure.
- Three-hole-punched 8½ by 11-inch calendar for September through December (easily found on most computers).
- 7-tab dividers.
- 5 or more clear page protectors.
- Notebook paper.

Set up your notebook in the following order.

- Plastic pocket to keep holiday receipts in. No more searching drawers and your purse for a store receipt when a gift needs to be returned.

- Tab #1 labeled *Calendar and Check List*. Behind it place the Holiday Inventory Sheet from pages 231 and 233 in the appendix. This will help to walk you through what items are needed for this busy time of year.

- Calendar pages for September–December. Record target dates for tasks, such as addressing Christmas cards, decorating the house, purchasing the tree, shopping and wrapping presents, writing thank-you notes. You may want to record each family member's holiday activities in different colors.

- Tab #2 labeled *Family Gifts*. On notebook paper record what items you purchase for your immediate and extended family.

- Tab #3 labeled *Other Gifts*. Record gifts to purchase or make for teachers, coaches, neighbors, friends, and others. Think quantity. Why not give the same thing to everyone? Simplify, simplify, simplify!

- Tab #4 labeled *Christmas Cards and Mailings*. Keep a list of addresses of people you'll mail cards or packages to. Or use clear page protectors to hold printed address labels and return address labels.

- Tab #5 labeled *Decorating Ideas*. Insert several page protectors designed so you can slip in magazine clippings of decorating ideas you come across and want to try.

- Tab #6 labeled *Holiday Food*. In a few clear page protectors, record your family's favorite holiday recipes or tuck in some you've found in magazines or newspapers. Use full sheet page protectors or ones designed to hold photos to house your recipe cards.

- Tab #7 labeled *Thank-You Notes*. Record any gifts received that need a thank you. I like to write thank-you notes on New Year's Day, the same time I transfer birthday and anniversary dates to my new calendar.

As with other ideas in this book, customize it to suit your fancy. Maybe you'll keep track of the Christmas cards you send and receive each year. Maybe you'll log in what gifts you gave to avoid repeats in the future. Make it yours!

Keeping Your Ducks in a Relative Row

We've taken a look at the most difficult aspect of organization—maintenance. Many moms, especially at the start of a new year, vow to get their acts together. The trick is *keeping* your act together once you've gotten it that way.

The trouble is…life happens. Dishes get used, towels become soiled, sheets need changing, homework has to be done, and refrigerators empty. If only we could be thankful all the time for the flurry of activity that takes place within our homes. Instead, we grumble about all the mess that ensues. We're human. We might as well face it: Our homes and schedules aren't going to stay magically organized unless we work to make it happen. We need to keep readjusting and realigning, all the while accepting that our homes won't stay picture perfect. We must keep plugging away at our routines. They're our best tool for maintaining order.

And remember that often God's agenda for our day isn't the same as ours. The more we keep quiet hearts and spirits and are thankful for life's little mishaps and interruptions—however daily they may be—the better moms we'll be.

I have a quote by one of my all-time favorite authors, Elisabeth Elliot, posted at my kitchen sink. It brings calm to my life and helps keep me centered, especially when circumstances are not going my way. It reads:

> The difference is Christ in me, not me in a different set of circumstances.

Longing to change your circumstances? Try changing your attitude instead. It really is the only thing we have any control over anyway.

What Works for Me

Jody Antrim, Illinois

Sometimes my children and I wanted to watch a favorite TV show but had some unfinished housekeeping chores. If the chores were fairly small tasks—things that could be accomplished in 15 minutes if done with full attention—I found a way to have them done well *and* with a good attitude. First we clarified what tasks still needed to get done (my list too!). Then we sat down to watch our show *but* worked like maniacs during commercials. The second the show went to a commercial, we leaped from the couch and scurried to see how much we could get done during those few minutes. It was amazing what we could accomplish!

The kids sometimes returned to the living room panting from going into high-energy mode. Sort laundry, clean the bathroom, vacuum a room, empty a dishwasher, empty trash cans from the rooms in the house—you name it and it could be accomplished during commercials. The kids did a good job, and we had the fun of watching a favorite TV show together.

My kids are grown now, but I *still* use that method when I'm not inspired to do menial tasks. My daughter, now a mom herself, says she still does it too. I have a feeling when my little grandchildren get old enough, they'll join in the fun.

What Works for Me

Kelly Hovermale, Michigan

To encourage my children to help with the laundry, they each have their own drawstring laundry bag for dirty clothes. They chose the fabrics—sports-themed, camouflage, or something pretty for a princess—and I sewed the bags. Children take more ownership when they have some say in the process.

What Works for Me

Pam Comstock, Michigan

Keep everyone's socks in the front closet by the shoes or wherever you exit and enter your house regularly. Then, when it's time to go somewhere, your children are not searching for socks. You also don't "lose" the kids when they go upstairs to get socks from their dressers and end up playing instead. As a mother of five, I speak from personal experience!

What Works for Me

Leigh Gray, North Carolina

Doing housework can be a daunting task. I would love for my house to be all clean at least one day of the week, but with life's demands and four active kids it's just not possible. This is something I've come to accept. I was willing for a while to change priorities just so my house was clean, but no one was happy, including me. So I have come to an agreement with myself (because I can be my worst enemy) that my house doesn't need to be totally clean even one day a week.

I decided to divide the chores into weekly jobs: vacuum on Monday, laundry on Tuesday, etc. Yes, that is right. Tuesday is the only day I do laundry. I have also come to the realization that my son doesn't have to have a spotless uniform at every baseball game where he is undoubtedly going to slide into base! Plus, I think his spotless uniform is more about me trying to look like the perfect mom than me wanting him to look clean.

For motivating myself to do housework, I take things in stride and spread it out. For those chores I don't have a liking for—almost all of them—I put on my headphones, turn on the music, and just get busy. I have also been known to put a timer on to see if I can beat the clock. Other times I ask my husband to take the kids to the park so I can get a job done without interruptions. He is very willing. He appreciates clean toilets as well!

What Works for Me

Marielle Hersey, Georgia

Needless to say, I definitely have a problem with organization. When something works for me, however, it really works!

I have three children whose stuff mysteriously appears all over the house. Nobody knows for sure how the items get there, and the kids forget to pick them up. That's when I decided to develop the "24-hour baskets."

I have a basket for each child. Whenever I find something that's out of place, I put it in the appropriate child's basket. If it's still in the basket the next day, it disappears forever. This may seem harsh, but it only took one time of disappearing toys to sharpen the children's memory and cleaning ability.

Note: If it's a very valuable item to the child, you can always regift it to him or her instead of throwing it out or donating. Imagine how surprised and thankful your child will be at her next birthday to see her toy reappear. You can also hold a treasure hostage until the child earns it back through doing extra chores.

What Works for Me

Piper Fountain, Michigan

When everyday chores needed to be done, it was much easier to do it myself, but I resisted this to fulfill my duty as mother and *train* my children instead. Young children love to help and love to please mom and dad. We parents are wise to take advantage of this (temporary) natural tendency. Although it takes more time at first and is imperfect (and to be honest, often not helpful at all), their willingness to learn household chores can really pay off later.

I have five children, so I made five general chores: set the table, clear the table, take out the trash and recycling, empty the dishwasher, and vacuum the downstairs. They were simple yet well defined. For example, the table clearer knew his job was to be done immediately after dinner, and that it included rinsing off and loading the dishes into the dishwasher. In addition, leftovers needed to be put into smaller containers, and pots and pans had to be washed. (The jobs became more complicated as the children grew older and were more able.)

The chores were posted on a chart on the fridge, and I rotated them every month or so. That proved to be enough time to train them well in their specific tasks. Jobs were not switched until each child mastered theirs fairly well. Our inspirational Scripture at the top of our job chart was Colossians 3:23: "Whatever you do, work at it with all your heart, as working for the Lord, not for men."

If tasks were not performed as expected, the kids earned "an extra job" for each infraction. These were creative things, such as cleaning the vegetable drawer in the refrigerator, washing the patio door windows, sweeping off the front porch, giving the dog a bath, folding a load of laundry. This worked surprisingly well. Extra jobs were also awarded if there was any whining or complaining about doing the chores. In this way I avoided nagging and lecturing and almost looked forward to the day when someone complained or forgot to do a job.

From the Heart of a Kid

If you want kids to help with chores, give them clear directions. I know from experience that being vague and saying something like "Clean up this place!" only makes kids frustrated. Maybe give them small jobs or teach them bigger jobs in steps. Don't overwhelm them, such as giving your six-year-old the job of cleaning the whole bathroom!

Keep an eye on them too. I remember one time I begged my mom to let me dust with a feather duster. I was probably six or seven. I was dusting way up high and couldn't see anything that was on top of the tall dresser. Apparently there was a lit candle there, and the feather duster caught fire. It wasn't good! However, my mom stayed kind of calm, put it out, and assigned me something else.

When your kids are younger, you'll probably have to follow after them and redo everything they do, but let them help anyway. When they're young, they just want to help, and if you don't start at an early age, when they get older they won't think they ever have to work. Here are some kid chores to start your little ones off:

- Let them "dust" using one of dad's old athletic socks. Mom always has kids use a cleaner that can be used on wood and glass in case they overspray.

- Children can hold a dustpan and sweep large spaces with a broom. Teach them to watch the other end of the broom when moving around the room. I remember when my brother almost took out our dining room window.

- Let them pull up a chair and rinse and stack dishes. You might not want to have them wash the good china.

- Kids can sort silverware as it comes out of the dishwasher. But take out all the sharp items first.

- Teach them to make a bed by making half yourself and having them try to get the other side to match.

- They can sort socks and fold dish towels and wash-cloths.

- Have them straighten shoes or boots in the entryway.

And remember to be their cheerleader and tell them what a great job they are doing. There is nothing sweeter to a child's ears than a mother's praise!

☺ Mackenzie

MOM'S TEN COMMANDMENTS
OF CLUTTER BUSTING

• •

1. If you got it out, put it away.

2. If you eat, open, or unwrap it, toss the wrapping, peel, or paper in the trash.

3. When you walk in the door, don't put your stuff down; put it away.

4. When your clothes are dirty, put them in the hamper. The floor is not a hamper.

5. Deal with your own papers or you will be issued a fine.

6. If you see something out of place and are walking anywhere near where it really belongs, be nice. Pick it up and take it back to its home.

7. If you open a door, drawer, or cupboard, shut it.

8. Clean up after yourself after you shower. Towels don't belong on the floor, but on the towel rack. Toothpaste cleans up great with wet toilet tissue. Would it kill you to wipe down a mirror?

9. Unfinished projects do not belong out in the common quarters. Take them to your room.

10. Be strict with yourself but gracious to others. And don't forget to smile and say please and thank you.

$$\textbf{11}$$

TAKING IT HOME, MAKING IT YOURS

• •

Whenever I give a weekend seminar on how a mom can get and stay organized in the midst of kids and chaos, I like to hear what women are thinking as we wind down our time together. Usually moms fall in one of two camps. In the first camp are the gals who are so motivated and energized they can't wait to get home, dejunk their houses, and whip everyone and everything into orderly shape. And they want it all done by next Tuesday. In the other camp are the gals whose heads are spinning and minds are reeling from processing so much information in the short time of a weekend seminar.

Thankfully, you have this weekend workshop in printed form. You can take all the time you need to process the information. May I gently suggest that both outlooks need to be somewhat tempered. The best approach to processing the information you have received is right up the middle.

To you gung-ho gals who are ready to implement all of this in a week's time, I say, "Whoa, Nellie!" You will drive everyone in your life nuts, especially the dear members of your family with whom you dwell. You won't get totally organized in a week or two. Remember, I have been learning, applying, failing, and retrying these ideas and systems for two decades now, and I am *still* not organized 100 percent of the time. In fact, I don't know any woman who is.

A few years back I was slated to appear alongside one of my favorite authors on the subject of home organization. She has mentored me through her dozens of books, and I really looked forward to observing her that weekend at the conference. I knew her talk would be flawless, her book table would operate smoothly, and the entire experience for her would go off without a hitch.

I was taken aback when she asked me to run to the store to purchase something she'd forgotten for her talk. Then she discovered she'd also forgotten her cash box and change. She had to use a shoebox and was digging through her purse making change from her coins. That experience was a big lesson for me. I learned, as I saw her handle those oversights with humor and ease, that striving to be perfect all the time is a terrible goal. Only God never makes mistakes. And trying to be God is exactly what caused Satan, who used to be an angel, to fall.

That weekend this well-seasoned mentor was such an inspiration. She was real. She made mistakes. She didn't try to appear to be perfect. Believe me, if anyone on earth could do it, she could. So relax and be real. Yes, you're excited to get started. Yes, you are inspired to rid your home of unwanted clutter and your schedule of unwanted commitments. You revel in the thought of having a smooth-running kitchen and a tidy abode for your family. Just keep your focus. Think back to the beginning of our time together when I talked about crafting a mission statement for your mothering. If you skipped that part, I forgive you. But go back and do it now. It will keep the reason you are becoming organized in the forefront of your mind.

Just what is the reason to maintain a relatively smooth-running and restful home? Well, it's not to wow the world around you with your organizational skills. It's not to keep your sanity by keeping a clean and clutter-free home (although that is a side benefit!). It's to have time for the important things in family life; to have a close, personal relationship with your Creator; to draw God's Word into every aspect of life; and to ultimately tie your children's heartstrings to God.

To you women who feel completely overwhelmed: Calm down. Take a deep breath. Clear your mind and think "baby steps." We are not talking about a one-year-old who's taking her first wobbly steps suddenly being entered in the Boston Marathon. Think about it. Even those runners who have crossed the finish line were once tottering tots. If you're afraid that getting your home and your time under control is too daunting, break it down into chunks. Pick one area to focus on for the next few weeks or months. Once you've formed new habits in that area and the skills become part of your regular routine, tackle another area.

I have seen women so weighed down at the thought of all the changes they wanted made that they were paralyzed. Then they calmed down and began by focusing on one simple area. They started by having a printed grocery list posted on the fridge and training their family members how to use it. After a month or so of trying out this suggestion, they found that their shopping and cooking began to sail along quite nicely. And as an added bonus, it freed up time in their busy schedules because they were no longer running to the grocery store four and five times a week. With the extra time, they began to dejunk their homes, one room per week.

After a couple of months they discovered, as they looked back on the time that had passed since the seminar, that two areas of their homes had changed. Their houses were less cluttered and their grocery shopping was more organized. As they adjusted to the "new" normal in their lives, a month or so later they'd get out their notes from the weekend and choose another area to take on.

One of the biggest thrills I receive from my speaking and writing ministry is seeing the amazing transformation in some of these women. Often they stop by my book table at a conference a year or two later. With joy in their hearts, and sometimes tears in their eyes, they tell their tales. So many have made radical changes in the way they manage their time and their homes. And all of them tell me it was a gradual process. I've yet to have any woman say, "I went home and put all your suggestions in place the first week." I guess if there is such a woman out there, *she* should be writing this book!

Even more astounding than the feedback I have received from these gals has been the responses of many husbands. I have gotten e-mails from men who have said their homes were wrecks before their wives signed up to take my mini workshop on organization. They are so thankful that another mom—*who herself struggles to stay organized*—came alongside their wives and gently led them out of lives of chaos. They tell me their kids are better for it and that the atmosphere of their homes has radically changed too. One delighted dad even wanted my home address so he could send me a dozen roses. (I suggested he give them to his newly organized wife instead.)

You see, we don't always realize the impact moms have on their entire families. Our planning, or lack thereof, affects those we love the most, both for good and for bad. Losing a child's permission slip, failing to have anything to feed our dear husbands before they leave for a hard day's work, letting the house get to the disaster stage on the night our teen wants to have a few friends sleep over causes stress. When you live alone and you are always a day late and a dollar short, dwelling in an apartment-turned-pigpen usually only affects you. When you live such a lifestyle as a mother in a family, it's a different ball game. Others will be directly affected by your poor time and home management.

So let's commit together to sticking to the tasks at hand. Will *our* to-do lists have every item crossed off at the end of each day? No. But God's agenda for our days can get done. Will our homes get physically organized and *stay* that way continually? No, but we can find flexible routines and workable plans for maintaining order most of the time. Will we ever truly "arrive"? Nope. Remember, the most important issue is the direction we're headed: toward calm and order or into disarray amid chaos.

And recall too, dear mom, the reason to get organized is not to add more "stuff" to your already crowded schedule. I used to measure success by how many activities I was involved in, how many "hats" I wore at church, and how much of my to-do list I'd crossed off at the end of the day. Then a wise mentor, my friend Debi, took me aside one day and told me of a different measuring stick. Do you know how I measure my life now? By how often I am reading out loud to our youngest child. You see, if my house is in relative order and I'm not overcommitted to activities and responsibilities outside of my home, I have time to sit and read a book to Spencer. We can curl up under a blanket and dive into the world of Narnia or wherever else he happens to want to go for the moment.

However, if my life is in chaos and I have too much on my plate, then reading aloud to my young son is the first thing to go. Or I'll notice that I feel irritated when my preteen, Mitchell, wants me to take a few minutes to listen to him practice his electric guitar. (And by that he means actually being in the same room with him, watching. I certainly can hear it from all corners of the house!) Or I'll notice that it has been quite a long time since I just flopped on Mackenzie's bed or in her beanbag chair to listen to the tales of her day at the home-school academy or her plans for next summer or her dreams for the future. Yep, when mom is too busy with outside commitments or too disorganized to keep on top of her home, downtime with the kiddos is the first thing to go.

Speaking Your Kids' Language

Take some time right now to think through what spells love to each of your kids. The short answer will be T-I-M-E, but just how does that play out for your particular children?

Do you have a little girl who cherishes tea parties with mom? Maybe she wants nothing more than for you to stop what you're doing, enter her world, and drink in some make-believe for a few unhurried moments. And by the way, Mom, looking at the clock or your watch every three minutes does not constitute unhurried. Believe me, I know.

My husband points out to me often just how much I peek at my watch or check the clock on the wall when I'm doing something the kids desire to do. Children pick up on this subtle cue and know we are anxious to move on to something "more important." We need to remember what it was like to be a child. Except for watching the clock at the end of the day at Delta Center Elementary School where I couldn't wait to see it hit 3:00 P.M. on weekdays, I really paid little attention to the clock. I played out in the neighborhood until I heard my mom call me home for supper. Bedtime was when mom announced it was time to curl my hair. (Yes, in those shocking pink sponge rollers!) Kids aren't as time oriented as adults are. We could take a cue from them once in a while. Why not take off our wrist-watches and just play?

Write your children's names and list two or three actions that speak love to that child. These are ways you could spend unhurried, one-on-one time with your kids that would mean the most to *them*. Then work to see how often you are able to make these times happen.

The Home Stretch

Now that you're at the end of this book, I pray you won't just set it on a shelf to collect dust. I hope it will be a manual you'll refer to again and again. After all, so much of this book now is you! You have recorded your well-thought-out goals, jotted down your areas of improvement, created priority lists, and really have, in the process, made this *your* book. Review and reread as you journey toward a life of relative rest and calm (as much as you can have in the midst of raising children!). I hope that in the months and years ahead this tool will be your GPS that keeps pointing you toward order and reminding you why you're trying to get there in the first place.

As I have grown, I've come to ask God for things I never thought of asking for in my younger years. As a schoolgirl I longed to grow up and leave home. I wanted so much to go to a Christian college, get a degree, and meet the man of my dreams, who would fall in love with me and marry me. Once I was married, I couldn't wait to have kids. Once the kids came along, I rushed their lives too. I was anxious for them to smile, talk, walk, ride a bike, and tie their shoes. But once the third child came along, something happened to me.

I had an immense desire to slow life down. Perhaps I sensed that because of my difficult pregnancies, Spencer might be the last child born into our family. Whatever the reason, I didn't rush his baby and his younger years so much. I cried terribly when he took his first steps. I didn't want him to start kindergarten. He didn't even learn to tie his shoes until he was eight. No more rushing to beat the cousins or even the baby in the book. (You know, those "what baby ought to be doing when" statements in raising baby books.)

I've started to realize just how short time is, and how we aren't promised tomorrow with our children. Have you ever thought about that? I consider the possibility that we may not have another chance to read the favorite book or play the best board game or have a good conversation. Our precious children could be taken from us suddenly by an illness or accident. Or they could move into young adulthood and discover God has plans for them that involve situations of danger, such as on the mission field or battlefield. Or something might happen to us. I know I don't want to look back near the end of my life with regret because I lived at one of two extremes.

I don't want to feel that my ducks were always perfectly in a row but spending unhurried time with my kids was not a part of our family's picture. But I also don't want to look back with sadness at the way I let life happen in a haphazard, come-what-may manner that resulted in a home full of chaos and disorder as family members fended for themselves.

Rather, I'd like to believe that I'll say I did the best with the time and resources allotted to me. That I attempted to take care of the "have-to's" of life in an efficient manner so I could get to all the "want to's" of life. That I was never too focused on myself and my agenda to hear the gentle whisper of God as he gave me different marching orders for my day than I had planned.

My prayer for you is that you'll make time for the important things in life, the things others will remember about you when you're gone. That you are a mom who reads to her kids, a true friend who allows her schedule to be interrupted for ministry to others, a caring neighbor with casserole in hand, a devoted wife who lets her husband know he is her priority. But most important, that you put God at the center of your life. May he assist and guide you in your quest to be a mom who gets her act together and, in the process, blesses those within her sphere of influence with her time, talents, and touch.

I am praying for you. You can do it!

• • • • • • • • From the Heart of a Kid • • • • • • • •

Once your ducks are in a row, how do you keep your little quackers from knocking them all down again? That is the tricky part. With little ones, sometimes it can't be prevented. With us older kids I say make it a family affair. Make deals with your kids: "If you do this, then here's what your reward will be." Some kids don't care if the house is a mess. Others get embarrassed if it is when their friends come over. Sometimes when we want to have friends over, we have to chip in and help in order to make it happen. Take this weekend for instance. My mom has been working nonstop on this book today. The Super Bowl is tomorrow, and we want to have some families over. She told us that if we wanted to have a Super Bowl party, we have to clean the house. The promise of a Super Bowl party makes us want to get to work. Even my brothers will pitch in and happily clean for that.

O.K., so here's the bottom line: Getting the family organized should be a team effort. Since you all live in the house, everyone should take part in cleaning it. Work together to keep your time in control. Each person should try not to lose papers, miss or be late for appointments, or forget to return the movies to the video store. It's just like when playing a sport. If everyone just stood there during a football game, and one person tried to take on the entire opposing team, that person would get creamed. When the family doesn't pitch in, they end up with a wiped out mom.

And make being a kid in your family enjoyable. Be encouraging as your kids try to help. Praise them for jobs well done or at least for the shot they gave it. Let them know you love your life. That even though sometimes the house and schedule are crazy, you wouldn't trade being their mom for anything in the world.

Happy organizing!

☺ Mackenzie

APPENDIX

● ●

This is your hands-on section, Mom. It showcases some easy, family-pleasing recipes for you to try on your crowd. I've included shortcuts when appropriate and steps such as freezing some of your leftovers for busy days.

Any time an idea has been mentioned that needs a form or sample, it's included here. Use any or all of these forms. And plan ahead. Don't run off one printed grocery list. Make enough to get you through several weeks or months. If you desire to use the daily to-do list, make multiple copies so you won't have to make a new one each day. Start setting up a holiday notebook early in the year. Maybe it could be one of your summertime projects. Remember, being organized boils down to being prepared.

RECIPES

Rounding Out Your Recipes

Fasten your apron strings and get out your pans, ladies! Here are some easy recipes to give your cooking a boost.

• • • • • • • • • • • **BREAKFAST** • • • • • • • • • • • •

Overnight Coffee Cake

Contributed by Melinda Walker, South Carolina

⅔ cup butter
1 cup white sugar
½ cup brown sugar
2 eggs
2 cups flour
1 teaspoon baking soda
½ teaspoon salt
1 teaspoon baking powder
1 teaspoon cinnamon
1 cup buttermilk
1 teaspoon vanilla

Topping
¾ cup nuts
¾ cup brown sugar

Cream together first four ingredients and set aside. Sift together the next five dry ingredients. Add buttermilk, vanilla, and dry ingredients alternately to creamed mixture. Pour into greased and floured 9 x 13-inch pan.

Mix topping ingredients and sprinkle over top.

Cover and refrigerate overnight.

Bake 30 to 40 minutes at 350 degrees.

Serve with a breakfast meat and fruit or juice.

Serves 12.

Kallie's Puffy Apple Pancake

Contributed by Pam Sischo, Michigan

2 tablespoons butter
3 eggs
½ cup flour
½ cup milk
½ teaspoon salt

Apple Topping ingredients
2 Granny Smith apples, peeled, cored, and sliced thin
¾ cup apple or white grape juice
2 tablespoons sugar
½ teaspoon cinnamon
¼ cup raisins (if desired)
2 tablespoons cornstarch
2 tablespoons cold water
2 teaspoons butter

Put butter in medium-size cast-iron skillet. Put skillet into a preheated 400-degree oven until butter is melted. Meanwhile, beat eggs in a medium bowl with an electric mixer for 30 seconds. Add flour, milk, and salt. Beat until smooth. Pour mixture into the hot skillet. Bake for 25 minutes or until puffed up and brown.

Apple Topping

Combine sliced apples, juice, sugar, cinnamon, and raisins in a sauce pan. Bring to a boil, and simmer until apples are tender.

In a separate small bowl stir together cornstarch and 2 tablespoons cold water. Pour into apple mixture and stir until thick and bubbly. Cook for two minutes. Stir in an additional 1 or 2 teaspoons of butter.

Serve warm over puffy oven pancake, along with meat and fruit for a complete breakfast. Great as a dessert or snack too!

Serves 4.

● ● ● ● ● ● ● ● ● ● ● **MAIN EVENT** ● ● ● ● ● ● ● ● ● ● ●

Easy No-Boil Italian Manicotti

This is a snap because you assemble it with the noodles uncooked!

½ pound ground sirloin
½ teaspoon each basil, oregano, and garlic powder
1 medium onion, finely chopped
1 28-ounce jar spaghetti sauce
    (or 3½ cups homemade spaghetti sauce)
2¼ cups water
Nonstick cooking spray
2 egg whites, lightly beaten
2½ cups ricotta cheese
⅓ cup parmesan cheese
1½ cups mozzarella cheese
1 box manicotti noodles (14 large noodles)

In a skillet, brown meat with spices and onion. Combine with spaghetti sauce and water in a large bowl.

Spray a 9 x 13-inch pan with nonstick cooking spray.

Spread in half the meat sauce mixture.

Mix egg whites and cheeses in a bowl and place in a gallon-size bag with a zip closure. Squeeze air out of bag and close. Snip a small hole in one corner of the bag. One by one, fill uncooked shells with the cheese mixture by squeezing it into the tubular shells, filling them from both ends to make it easier. Place in pan (they *will* fit!) and cover evenly with remaining meat sauce. Seal tightly with foil. Bake at 350 degrees for 1½ hours.

Let stand 10 minutes before serving.

Serves 6 to 8.

Make-ahead shortcut: Brown meat with spices and onion. Cool, place in freezer bag, and freeze. Fill the noodles with egg-and-cheese mixture and freeze in one layer in a gallon-size freezer bag. On cooking day, assemble the dish as directed, adding 15 to 20 minutes to the cooking time.

Chicken Taco Rice
Contributed by Melinda Walker, South Carolina

A new twist on a traditional flavor kids love!

1 pound boneless, skinless chicken breast, cubed
   (about 3 cups cooked)
2 tablespoons oil
1 14-ounce can chicken broth
1 4-ounce can tomato sauce
1 package taco seasoning
1 15-ounce can corn, drained
1 small green or red bell pepper, cut into strips
1½ cups instant rice (white or brown)
Taco chips
1 cup cheddar cheese, shredded
Sour cream

In a skillet, brown chicken in oil until tender. Add broth, tomato sauce, and taco seasoning. Bring to a boil, cover, and reduce heat. Simmer 5 minutes. Add corn and bell pepper. Return to boil. Add rice, cover, and remove from heat. After 5 minutes fluff with fork and serve over crumbled taco chips.

Top with cheese and sour cream.

Serves six.

Make-ahead shortcut: Chop leftover cooked chicken. Package in 3-cup portions and place in zipper bags in the freezer. Do the same with the green or red pepper. They may be cut and frozen without cooking or blanching first.

Ham Turnovers
Amy O'Quinn, Georgia

1½ cups chopped ham
1 3-ounce package cream cheese, softened (or slightly less than half an 8-ounce package)
1 tablespoon milk
1 tablespoon butter
2 cans crescent rolls

Combine first 4 ingredients, and spoon onto 8 triangles of crescent rolls. Place another triangle of dough on top. Stretch and seal edges well, forming a turnover.

Bake on ungreased cookie sheet at 350 degrees for 16 to 18 minutes or until rolls are golden brown.

Makes 8.

Taco Crescents
Amy O'Quinn, Georgia

1 pound ground beef
1 package taco seasoning
1 8-ounce can tomato sauce
1 cup mozzarella cheese
2 cans crescent rolls

In a skillet, brown beef and drain well. Stir in seasoning mix and tomato sauce. Stir in cheese. Place half in a freezer bag, label and freeze to use another day. With the remaining mixture, place a heaping tablespoon of mixture on each crescent-roll triangle. Roll up in a traditional crescent shape.

Bake on ungreased cookie sheet at 350 degrees for 16 to 18 minutes or until golden brown.

Makes 16.

• • • • • • • • • • • • • **SOUPS** • • • • • • • • • • • • • •

Hamburger Soup
Contributed by Pam Sischo, Michigan

If you brown some beef and freeze in one-pound portions, you'll have a jump-start on this easy soup!

1 pound lean ground beef
2 packages onion soup mix
2 beef bouillon cubes
4 to 6 cups water
4 potatoes, peeled and cubed
4 carrots, peeled and diced
1 15-ounce can corn, drained
other vegetables as desired

Brown beef in large pot. Stir in onion soup mix, beef bouillon cubes, and water. Add potatoes and carrots. Bring to a boil and cook over medium-low heat until vegetables are tender. Just before serving, stir in corn as well as any other vegetables you may like. Season with salt and pepper to taste.

Serves 4 to 6.

Recipe may be doubled, and it reheats beautifully.

Note: Once in a while I add a 15-ounce can of diced tomatoes and/or 2 tablespoons of Worcestershire sauce for a change of flavor.

Chicken–Spinach Tortellini Soup

Will kids really eat spinach? Sure, in this delicious, easy soup. Freeze leftover chicken in two-cup portions to make creating this a snap.

1 tablespoon olive oil
1 onion, chopped
1 clove garlic, minced (or 1 teaspoon chopped garlic)
8 cups chicken broth (or 8 cups water and 4 or more bouillon
     cubes to taste)
10 ounces frozen, chopped spinach
2 cups diced, cooked chicken
14 ounces petite, diced tomatoes (or 14 ounces tomato puree if
     your kids don't like chunks)
1 tablespoon dried basil
1 teaspoon oregano
½ teaspoon salt
1 package refrigerated, cheese-stuffed tortellini
fresh, grated parmesan cheese (optional)

In a large kettle, sauté onion in oil until tender. Add all the remaining ingredients except tortellini. Simmer 20 minutes. Add tortellini and simmer 15 minutes more until cooked.

Top with fresh grated parmesan cheese.

Serves 6.

● ● ● ● ● ● ● ● ● ● **THIS AND THAT** ● ● ● ● ● ● ● ● ● ●

Ranch Dressing

1 cup real mayonnaise
⅔ cups buttermilk
2 tablespoons whole milk (or a little more to thin, if needed)
1 teaspoon salt
½ teaspoon black pepper

1 teaspoon each dried celery leaves and parsley
½ teaspoon oregano
2 tablespoons finely minced green onion (or 1 teaspoon dried
   minced onion)
2 teaspoons lemon juice
2 teaspoons sugar

Whisk the ingredients together and store chilled in the refrigerator
for up to one week.

This ranch recipe is versatile. Use as a sauce, dressing, or dip. Yum!

Honey Mustard

2 cups mayonnaise (low-fat works fine)
½ cup prepared mustard
½ cup honey
¾ cup brown sugar
1 tablespoon dried parsley (optional)

Combine the ingredients and keep in a covered container in the refrigerator for up to two weeks.

Use as a salad dressing or for dipping chicken nuggets. Kids love it!

Marsha O's Popcorn
Contributed by Pam Sischo, Michigan

A simple, sweet snack for a lazy family night!

1 stick butter
18 large marshmallows
¾ cup brown sugar
8 to 10 cups popped popcorn

Melt first three ingredients together over low heat in large pan. Stir in 8 to 10 cups popped popcorn. Remove from heat. Pour into a bowl and enjoy!

• • • • • • • • • • DESSERTS • • • • • • • • • • •

Blueberry Buckle

Contributed by Marybeth Whalen, North Carolina

This recipe can pull double duty. It also makes a great breakfast dish.

2 cups flour
¾ cup sugar
2½ teaspoons baking powder
¾ teaspoon salt
¼ cup butter, melted
¾ cup milk
1 egg
2 cups blueberries (fresh or frozen)

Streusel Topping
½ cup sugar
⅓ cup self-rising flour
½ teaspoon cinnamon
¼ cup melted butter

Mix all ingredients, folding in blueberries last. Pour into greased and floured 8-inch square pan. (You may use a nonstick cooking spray with flour such as Baker's Joy or PAM For Baking.)

Combine topping ingredients and spread on top of blueberry mixture.

Bake at 375 degrees for 45 to 50 minutes.

Serves 6 to 8.

Make-ahead shortcut: In the summer when they are cheaper, freeze blueberries in two-cup portions. Prepare quart-size bags with the buckle's dry ingredients and sandwich-size bags with the streusel dry ingredients. Store in freezer. You'll be halfway to this delicious dish, saving you time and mess on a busy day.

White-Chocolate Raspberry Cheesecake
Thais VanGinhoven

I had to feature this decadent dessert from my sister-in-law Thais. She's been hired to make this confection, requested to donate it to charity auctions, and my kids always hope she serves it when we go to her house. The taste is incredible, and you can make it 2 to 3 days ahead or wrap it well and freeze it for up to a month—if it's not eaten before then.

Crust
1 cup flour
½ cup butter, softened
3 tablespoons sugar

Mix together ingredients with a fork until crumbly. Press flat in a 10-inch springform pan. Bake 10 minutes at 350 degrees. Do not overcook!

Remove from oven and set aside to cool.

Raspberry Sauce
1 10-ounce package frozen raspberries
1 tablespoon cornstarch

Heat ingredients in a pan over medium heat until it boils and thickens, about 5 minutes.
Set aside to cool slightly.

Cheese Filling
4 8-ounce packages cream cheese, softened
½ cup sugar
1 cup heavy cream, unwhipped
2 teaspoons vanilla
2 eggs, whisked
10 ounces white chocolate, melted and then cooled slightly

Melt the white chocolate in the microwave or in a pan on the stove over very low heat. Set aside and let cool slightly.

In a large bowl, blend cheese and sugar well. Alternately add the cream, vanilla, and eggs, beating well after each addition. Gently fold in melted white chocolate.

To assemble cheesecake:
Spread half the cheese filling on top of the crust.

Top with half the raspberry mixture.

Take a butter knife and swirl the two together.

Repeat the layers one more time with remaining cheese filling and raspberry sauce. Swirl again. It makes a beautiful design!

Bake covered lightly with tin foil for 10 minutes at 450 degrees. Then turn oven down to 250 degrees and remove foil. Bake 1 hour. Cake will be very moist! Turn off oven and leave cake inside for 2 hours.

Remove and refrigerate, loosely covered, for at least 8 hours before serving.

Serves 16 to 20.

When serving, get a large serving platter and place a paper doily on it. Remove the sides of the springform pan and place entire cake on platter. Add pizzazz by topping with raspberries and edible flowers (pansies that have been rinsed and patted dry work great). Enjoy!

FORMS

MY MISSION AS A MOM

● ●

_____

_____

_____

_____

_____

_____

_____

_____

_____

_____

_____

_____

Signed _____ Date _____

DAILY
TO-DO LIST

I can do all things through Christ who strengthens me.
PHILIPPIANS 4:13 NKJV

● ●

Have to do: _____

_____

_____

_____

Want to do: _____

_____

_____

_____

Contact e-mails: _____

_____

Contact phones: _____

_____

Write to: _____

_____

_____

Don't forget: _____

_____

_____

To buy: _____

_____

_____

_____

GROCERY LIST

PRODUCE
- Potatoes
- Onions
- Carrots
- Lettuce
- Tomatoes
- Celery
- Mushrooms
- Green pepper
- Spinach
- Broccoli
-
-

FRUIT
- Apples
- Bananas
- Oranges
- Lemons/limes
- Grapes
- Pears
- Peaches
- Plums
- Melon
-
-

BREADS
- Bread
- Hot dog buns
- Hamburger buns
- English muffins
- Bagels
- Pita bread
- Croutons
-
-
-

CANNED/DRY GOODS
- Tomato paste/ sauce
- Spaghetti sauce
- Tomatoes
- Salsa
- Olives, black or green
- Mushrooms
- Fruit cocktail
- Pineapple
-
-
-

PASTA/RICE
- Spaghetti
- Rotini
- Lasagna
- Macaroni
- Brown/white rice
-
-
-

CONDIMENTS
- Ketchup
- Mustard
- Relish
- Mayonnaise
- Soy sauce
- Vinegar
- Honey
- Salad dressing
-
-
-
-
-
-
-

BAKING SUPPLIES
- ○ Flour
- ○ Sugar
- ○ Yeast
- ○ Brown sugar
- ○ Cornstarch
- ○ Baking powder
- ○ Baking soda
- ○ Vanilla
- ○ Almond extract
- ○ Chocolate chips
- ○
- ○

SPICES
- ○
- ○
- ○
- ○
- ○

FROZEN FOODS
- ○ Orange Juice
- ○ Corn
- ○ Peas
- ○ Mixed vegetables
- ○ Lima beans
- ○
- ○
- ○
- ○
- ○

DAIRY
- ○ Milk
- ○ Creamer
- ○ Eggs
- ○ Butter
- ○ Cream cheese
- ○ Sour cream
- ○ Cottage cheese
- ○ Ricotta cheese
- ○ Cheddar
- ○ Mozzarella
- ○
- ○
- ○
- ○
- ○
- ○
- ○

MEATS
- ○ Ground beef
- ○ Bacon
- ○ Sausage
- ○ Ground turkey
- ○ Chicken
- ○
- ○
- ○
- ○
- ○

MISCELLANEOUS
- ○ Facial tissue
- ○ Napkins
- ○ Towels
- ○ Dishwasher soap
- ○ Dish soap
- ○ Bath soap
- ○ Toilet paper
- ○ Hand soap
- ○
- ○
- ○
- ○
- ○
- ○
- ○
- ○
- ○
- ○
- ○
- ○
- ○
- ○
- ○
- ○
- ○
- ○
- ○

HOLIDAY
INVENTORY SHEET

SHOPPING ESSENTIALS CHECKLIST

- ○ Christmas cards
- ○ Stamps
- ○ Mailing boxes
- ○ Mailing tape
- ○ Wrapping paper
- ○ Gift tags
- ○ Scotch tape
- ○ Ribbon/bows
- ○ Thank-you notes

PLANNING

1. When am I going to fill out my Christmas cards and/or write our Christmas letter?

2. How and when will I tackle wrapping presents? (Wrap one per night before bed? Have someone take the kids for a few hours on a Saturday? Hold a wrapping party?)

3. When will I make a trip to the post office or UPS? (Mail packages by December 10 so they'll arrive by Christmas.)

4. What fun traditions will we follow as a family this year?

5. Is there anything I need to purchase to make this happen?

6. What holiday foods will I prepare this year?

7. What do I need to purchase in order to make them?

8. How and when will we decorate our home this year?

9. Do I need to make any purchases to do this?

10. When will I write thank-you notes?

About the Author

Karen Ehman has been described as profoundly practical, engagingly funny, and downright real. She is a member of the Proverbs 31 Ministries national speaking team and a columnist for *Hearts at Home* monthly magazine. Karen actively participates in Hearts at Home Ministries by teaching workshops and being part of the drama team. She has a weekly radio spot called "The Keep It Simple Woman" on the WCIC family of radio stations in central Illinois.

The author of four women's books, including *A Life That Says Welcome: Simple Ways to Open Your Heart and Home to Others,* Karen was also the project creator of the Hearts at Home *Just for Mom's Planner.* She has been a guest on national television and radio programs including *The 700 Club, At Home Live, Engaging Women, The Harvest Show, Moody Midday Connection,* and Dr. James Dobson's *Focus on the Family.*

A graduate of Spring Arbor University, Karen is married to Todd, and they have three sometimes quarrelsome but mostly charming children: Mackenzie, Mitchell, and Spencer. Before motherhood, Karen was a teacher and cheerleading coach. Now she spends her days homeschooling, carpooling, and waiting in the volleyball bleachers and at little league stands. Though hopelessly craft-challenged with partially finished scrapbooks, she enjoys baking and cooking and has won several blue ribbon rosettes at county fairs for her cookies, cakes, pies, and breads.

Karen is a popular national speaker on topics that include home organization, hospitality, contentment, marriage, and motherhood. If you would like to discover more about her topics or contact her to speak at your conference or event, please go to:

www.KarenEhman.com

Hearts at Home

The Hearts at Home organization is committed to meeting the needs of women in the profession of motherhood. Founded in 1993, Hearts at Home offers a variety of resources and events to assist women in their jobs as wives and mothers.

Find out how Hearts at Home can provide you with ongoing education and encouragement in the profession of motherhood. In addition to this book, our resources include the *Hearts at Home* magazine, the Hearts at Home devotional, and our Hearts at Home website. Additionally, Hearts at Home events make a great getaway for individuals, moms' groups, or for that special friend, sister, or sister-in-law. The regional conferences, attended by more than 10,000 women each year, provide a unique, affordable, and highly encouraging weekend for the woman who takes the profession of motherhood seriously.

Hearts at Home
1509 N. Clinton Blvd.
Bloomington, IL 61701-0248
Phone: (309) 828-6667
Fax: (309) 829-8087
E-mail: hearts@hearts-at-home.org
Web: www.hearts-at-home.org

Other Great Books from Harvest House Publishers and Hearts at Home

BALANCE THAT WORKS WHEN LIFE DOESN'T
Susie Larson

Prepare healthy meals, exercise, rest, study and pray, serve, keep the household running, and even manage a career—how can you possibly balance all the demands of today's Christian lifestyle? Susie Larson encourages you to effectively respond and adjust by evaluating your core beliefs, your unique personality, and God's will for your life to discover how to make the best choices that create a natural, healthy flow and rhythm you can live with.

GOT TEENS?
Jill Savage and Pam Farrel

Jill Savage, founder of Hearts at Home Ministries, and Pam Farrel, cofounder of Masterful Living Ministries, can shout "Yes" to the question, "Got Teens?" They offer common-sense solutions, insightful research, and creative ideas to help you guide your children successfully into adulthood. As a mom, you don't have to be perfect, just prepared with practical, biblical tools to identify and develop each child's strengths, make choices over what kids can do and who with, and turn around destructive behavior or bad habits. *Got Teens?* can help! Discover how to best serve as defender, shepherd, CEO, or one of the other 12 vital roles.

MAMA SAID THERE'D BE DAYS LIKE THIS
Jenn Doucette

Are you running as fast as you can to keep up or to stay just ahead? Jenn Doucette offers a humorous, insightful look at how you can find much-needed rest stops by experiencing girl time, choosing contentment, setting boundaries to achieve freedom, getting a grip on emotions, and giving yourself a break. With comedic flair, Jenn confesses to her own failings as well as God's successes, reminding all mothers that it is healthy to laugh, take a break, and practice grace.

THE MOM I WANT TO BE
T. Suzanne Eller

Your experience as a mother is influenced by the mothering you received as a child. If neglect or difficulties were part of that upbringing, you need a fresh, healthy vision of motherhood as you face the responsibility of being a parent yourself. T. Suzanne Eller compassionately discusses how a woman can turn from a painful past and embrace a godly example of motherhood. She shares how a shattered legacy can be put back together, the path to restoring the broken image of motherhood, and ways to let go and embrace a new story. This book is a celebration of God's healing power.

MOTHERHOOD: THE GUILT THAT KEEPS ON GIVING
Julie Ann Barnhill

Julie Barnhill explores how guilt can keep moms from experiencing motherhood with joy. With her trademark honesty and humor, she eases you down from the top of "Mount Guiltmore" and into the freedom to be your own unique brand of mom by acknowledging the things you *don't* have guilt over and embracing those, understanding the inheritance from your own mother, and discovering personal qualities that will make you a *great* mom. Practical insights and a sassy, realistic look at all mothers do will give you a fresh perspective that will open your life to all God has for you and your children.

MY HEART'S AT HOME
Jill Savage

Founder and executive director of Hearts at Home, Jill Savage explores the important role "home" plays in a family's journey. With her personable, humorous style, Jill shares from her experience as a mother of five and from conversations with other moms to offer practical ideas and motivation to create homes that are safe places for families to blossom; community centers that offer hospitality and compassion; churches where prayer and Scripture guide all members; museums filled with a family's history, stories, and heritage; and schools that teach virtue, integrity, and ethics. Build the heart of your home on biblical principles and raise families that are strong, loving, and firmly on a foundation of faith.

ORDINARY MOM, EXTRAORDINARY GOD
Mary E. DeMuth

This heartfelt devotional provides a soothing respite amid the chaos of family life. Mary DeMuth creatively focuses on the gift of motherhood as she explores how you can rest quietly in the Lord even on crazy-busy days, be thankful for the duties as well as the joys of being a mom, and offer God a heart to prune so you bear good fruit. Personal stories, scriptural truth, and probing prayers help you remain connected to the most amazing and extraordinary Parent of all.

To learn more about Harvest House books
or to read sample chapters, log on to our website:

www.harvesthousepublishers.com

HARVEST HOUSE
PUBLISHERS